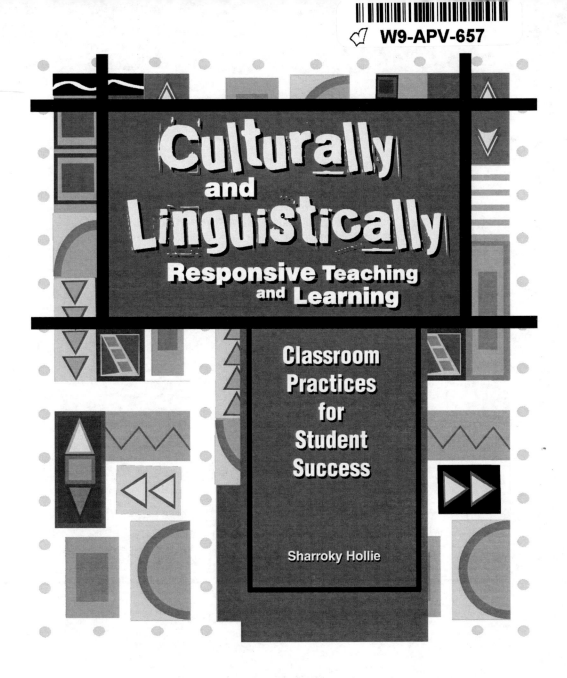

Culturally and Linguistically Responsive Teaching and Learning

Classroom Practices for Student Success

Sharroky Hollie

Author
Sharroky Hollie, Ph.D.

Foreword
Eugenia Mora-Flores, Ph.D.

SHELL EDUCATION

Publishing Credits

Dona Herweck Rice, *Editor-in-Chief*; Robin Erickson, *Production Director*;
Lee Aucoin, *Creative Director*; Timothy J. Bradley, *Illustration Manager*;
Sara Johnson, M.S.Ed., *Senior Editor*; Evelyn Garcia, *Associate Education Editor*;
Juan Chavolla, *Cover/Interior Layout Designer*; Corinne Burton, M.A.Ed., *Publisher*

Image credits

All photos courtesy of Baba Riley; p.146 Monkey Business images/Shutterstock

Shell Education
5301 Oceanus Drive
Huntington Beach, CA 92649-1030
http://www.shelleducation.com
ISBN 978-1-4258-0686-6
© 2012 by Shell Educational Publishing, Inc.

Table of Contents

Foreword

I am a firm believer that teachers enter the field of education with the intention of doing great things for all students. An environment where all children feel comfortable and capable of learning will be created and teachers will provide a curriculum and employ pedagogical approaches that facilitate high levels of academic achievement for all students. These aspirations are often discussed at a theoretical level and remain aspirations until teachers are equipped with the knowledge and strategies for successful teaching and learning.

In my own journey as a teacher, I can remember beginning the school year with the hopes that I would know how best to support the unique group of students I met each year. As I got to know my students, I was always amazed at the range of diversity they brought to the classroom. I was excited and a little nervous, wondering if I was equipped with the knowledge and strategies needed to serve them equally. Each year, I would turn to colleagues and mentors to help me through the challenges. My colleagues and I explored a variety of strategies, hoping they would work.

As I read this book, I feel empowered as a teacher, knowing I will have access to the practices needed to support diverse student populations. As I reread many chapters, I am reminded of multiple conversations with colleagues searching for answers. Through this book, Sharroky Hollie becomes that colleague: the person you can turn to when you need to understand the beauty of the diversity in your classroom. Not only does it provide the theoretical framework that helps teachers understand what diversity is, but also the practical strategies to support all learners.

This book is a conversation with Sharroky. He asks you to question your learning and to call upon your own expertise and extend your practices. I think we all believe in culturally responsive instruction and probably aspire to be culturally responsive teachers. This book helps novice *and* experienced teachers understand diversity and equips them with tools to build upon that diversity to reach high outcomes for all students. It is a not only a resource but also a necessary reminder about why we became teachers—to provide all students with a relevant, rigorous, and high quality education.

As a teacher educator, I am excited about the opportunity to share this book with my students. It has extended my understanding of culturally responsive instruction through a more holistic framework that incorporates linguistic diversity. Understanding the role of language in academic success is imperative for all teachers. This book clearly discusses culturally and *linguistically* responsive instruction. It explains that language diversity exists within a language as complexly as it does across languages, and that the language students bring to the classroom is an asset to be developed. There are a variety of strategies shared to help teachers understand language and support diverse language users.

At the beginning of the book, Sharroky tells of the personal importance of writing this book. It was a new chapter in a successful career that captured his passion as an educator. It was that *thing* we are drawn to do, and if we do not do it, as Sharroky shares, it "would haunt us for the rest of our lives." Reading this book is one of those moments for me and will be for many teachers. If we do not learn all we can about the diversity of our students and how to become culturally and linguistically responsive teachers, failing the many students we teach will indeed haunt us for the rest of our lives. I can assure you that reading through this book will equip you with the knowledge and strategies needed to support culturally and linguistically diverse students.

—*Eugenia Mora-Flores*, Ph.D.
Consultant, Author, and Associate Professor,
Rossier School of Education,
University of Southern California

Introduction

Most of us have had some goal, challenge, or feat that we want to accomplish in our personal or professional lives, and not having accomplished that challenge might have haunted us forever. Writing this book was one of my feats. As a teacher educator conducting professional development programs, teaching at the university, and cofounding a school, I developed a way of looking at culturally responsive teaching differently from many educators with whom I interfaced and in a way that was built on the outstanding scholarship and research done previously. As a doctoral candidate conducting research for my dissertation, I realized that while there was voluminous theory on culturally responsive teaching, there was very little in the research on the *practice* of culturally responsive teaching. There were few, if any, school-wide models or exemplary classrooms. When I researched or inquired where one could find culturally responsive teaching, there was a paucity of examples. At that point, the goal of my research became twofold: making the theory palatable for teachers in the classroom and creating exemplary classroom models around the country.

As other researchers and I developed the approach explained in this book, people would come up to me after one of my presentations or workshops and ask, "Do you have a book on this?" When I replied, "No," they would ask, "Why not?" and I did not have an adequate response. Colleagues in my field would praise me for the excellence of the work but admonish me for not writing it down. I did not recognize that what I was doing would not have credibility until it was in print. Editors would approach me and ask me to send a proposal and a draft of a chapter. But I never did.

For the past 15 years, I have been a teacher educator from three different vantage points. My first view is from an academic standpoint— an assistant professor in teacher education at California State University, Dominguez Hills. There, I have taught hundreds of preservice educators in the areas of classroom management, methodology, and reading. As a professor at a teacher-training institute, I have observed student and intern teachers in over 1,000 classrooms. The context for their learning to teach is in the urban schools whose students live in communities like Watts, South Los Angeles, Compton, Long Beach, and other Southern California school districts.

My second perspective is as a cofounder of a charter school, the Culture and Language Academy of Success (CLAS) in Los Angeles, founded in 2003. CLAS is a kindergarten through eighth grade laboratory school that incorporates culturally responsive pedagogy as its primary approach. My charge at CLAS is focused around the curriculum, instruction, and professional development. I have also been responsible for teacher development, specifically around teachers both new and veteran, to become culturally responsive. CLAS has become a national model for culturally responsive teaching.

My third vantage point has been from a national perspective as an expert in the field of culturally responsive pedagogy. This view has allowed my team and me to work with many schools and districts and thousands of teachers in their quest to be culturally responsive to better serve their underserved students. My advantage as a so-called expert has been in learning the range of the landscape of what one finds from classroom to classroom: the unevenness of the commitment to implement culturally responsive teaching at various districts and the highs and lows of the skill levels of the teachers. Regardless of whether I am observing an intern, designing a lesson-planning template for my school, or conducting training somewhere around the country, the convergence of the three perspectives is evident in this finding: *the need for culturally responsive teaching in every classroom.* From my three vantage points, I know that as educators, we are poised to meet this need and fulfill what I would now call a *moral imperative* to provide equitable and excellent education for all children.

My Goal in Writing This Book

The relevance of this book for educators is its focus on two aspects of culturally and linguistically responsive and relevant instruction. The first aspect is the focus on equity and diversity, which are addressed in the first two chapters. Chapters 1 and 2 specifically center on the sensitive issues of race, culture, and language by providing the reader with a laser focus on the complexity of culture and a variant perspective on language difference. The second aspect of the book concentrates on pedagogy, based on the premise that having discussions about teaching is just not sufficient to address the problems of underserved students. In order to be culturally responsive, transforming instructional practices must occur. Not only must educators think differently, but they must teach differently as well. Concrete activities and strategies are rolled out through five areas described fully in Chapters 3 though 7. The areas are classroom management, academic-literacy instruction, academic-vocabulary instruction, academic-language instruction, and creating a responsive learning environment. Based on my research, these are the areas that teachers and students are most in need of and represent the greatest possibility for change.

The purpose of this book is fairly simple and straightforward: it is to provide a universal framework to enable educators to change their mindsets and hearts about how students are looked upon culturally and linguistically. It also provides a pedagogical framework for infusing culturally and linguistically responsive teaching into instruction in every possible way. The first three chapters and the last chapter serve as bookends for the three practice-oriented chapters in the middle of the book. Chapters 1, 2, and 3 provide the context in which effective instruction for academic literacy, vocabulary, and language can take place as described in chapters 4, 5, and 6 respectively. Chapter 7 addresses the nature of a responsive learning environment and provides additional insights into the context necessary for effective instruction consistent with the principles established in the first three chapters.

Features of This Book

Fostering student engagement in learning activities is a primary goal for all teachers. Similarly, as I wrote this book, I wanted to provide features that would engage the reader in thinking about personal perspectives about culturally and linguistically responsive pedagogy. These features are designed to invite teachers to take a few minutes to reflect on the content and how they can incorporate the ideas into their professional learning experiences. Some suggestions may lead into conversations with their colleagues. The features found throughout the book include the following:

- Each chapter opens with an *Anticipation Guide*, which offers a number of statements related to the chapter topic. The guide invites teachers to specify whether they agree or disagree with each of the statements listed.

- At the end of each chapter is a *Reflection Guide*. This invites teachers to reconsider what they have read and their responses to the statements in the Anticipation Guide. Additionally, there are other reflection activities designed to enhance teachers' understanding of what happens in their own classroom in the context of culturally and linguistically responsive teaching.

- *Pause to Ponder* is another feature designed to engage teachers' attention on critical issues in their classroom, school, or district. These activities are presented to prompt exploration of their thoughts about the material and its relevance to their current situations.

- Sidebars are interspersed throughout the chapters. The terminology used in discussing culturally and linguistically responsive pedagogy is particularly important. Sidebars found throughout the book provide a model for the use of precise language in discussions. Definitions of important terms are also highlighted and included in sidebars.

- *Resources for Teachers*, a feature found in the appendices, presents a collection of practical, evidence-based instructional activities. My colleagues at CLAS and I have successfully used these activities, as have many of the teachers who have attended our professional development programs. This resource component also includes a Learning Environment Survey designed for collegial observations of the quantitative and qualitative aspects of the classroom.

My hope is that teachers come away from this book more culturally responsive in thought and in action.

Defining Culturally and Linguistically Responsive Pedagogy

◄□▷◄□▷ ◄□▷◄□▷ ◄□▷◄□▷

Chapter 1

Anticipation Guide

What do you think of when you encounter the term *culturally responsive teaching*? Do you agree or disagree with the following statements about the concept?

A_____ Culturally responsive teaching is meant to help with race relations among educators and students.

A_____ All students can achieve highly when given the opportunity to learn.

D_____ Racial identity and cultural identity are synonymous.

_____ Nonstandard English is a simplified version of Standard English.

D_____ Socioeconomic status is the most critical factor in student success.

◄□▷◄□▷ ◄□▷◄□▷ ◄□▷◄□▷

What's in a Name?

Unfortunately, the term *culturally responsive teaching* has become a cliché, buried in the grave of educational terms that are cast about like ghosts in books, state mandates, district initiatives, and conference themes. Two summers ago, I received an email from an educator in the Midwest who said that her superintendent had now branded the district "culturally responsive." However, she was not sure what that meant and needed to know immediately—before the proverbial one-day mandated district professional development program. Throughout my home state of California, many districts want to be culturally responsive, or at least they think they do. In reality, what they are seeking is how to address racial issues under the cover of *culturally responsive teaching*. And why not? The term sounds appropriate and informative, seems to cover the sensitive issues of race in a nonthreatening way, and serves a purpose in situations where the achievement gap persists and where negative attitudes about race, culture, and language remain stubborn. But turning the meaning of culturally responsive teaching into a quick fix for race relations, diversity issues, and achievement gap woes is a fleeting solution. The authenticity and relevance of the term is actually steeped in transforming instructional practices to make the difference for improving relationships between students and educators and increasing student achievement.

Multiple names and definitions have been given to culturally responsive teaching over the past 40 years. These variations include, among others, culturally responsive pedagogy, culturally compatible teaching, culturally relevant teaching, culturally connected teaching, culturally responsive learning, culturally matched teaching, cultural proficiency, and culturally appropriate teaching (Gay 2000). The multiple definitions of *culturally responsive teaching* have contributed to its clichéd use that has diluted its meaning. Furthermore, these superficial interpretations have led to obscure attempts at implementation in districts (focused on professional development), schools (focused on curriculum initiatives), and classrooms (focused on instructional strategies).

Think of almost any innovation that has had staying power in education and may still be in use today. The term for that innovation will not have changed, although its interpretation may have evolved in a consistent way. An example that comes to mind is *cooperative learning*, a concept put forth in the late 1960s (Johnson, Johnson, and Holubec 1994; Kagan and Kagan 2009). The term *cooperative learning* has remained intact for almost four decades and has furthermore evolved to include the concept *collaborative learning*. When most educators encounter the term *cooperative learning*, there is consensus on its meaning. My point is that cooperative learning has had staying power because it has not been subjected to multiple terms and interpretations, as is the case with culturally responsive teaching.

I believe that clarity can sometimes be more important than agreement. Being clear on what is meant by culturally and linguistically responsive teaching is certainly one of those cases. In training over 25,000 educators and speaking to hundreds of audiences across the country, I have found that most teachers and administrators appreciate the focus on clarity as opposed to forcing agreement.

What Does Culturally and Linguistically Responsive Teaching Mean?

For the purposes of my work and this book in particular, I advocate a singular use of the concept and terminology of culturally responsive teaching. If an educator desires to be culturally and linguistically responsive or a school is looking to implement the approach, I recommend that all stakeholders agree upon one term and one meaning—preferably the one used in this book. As a result of the work in which I have been immersed for the past 12 years, I have adopted the term *culturally and linguistically responsive pedagogy* (CLR). I settled on this term for the following three reasons:

1. I have found that many so-called followers of culturally responsive teaching are actually most interested in *racially* responsive teaching. There is a tendency to be more focused on racial identity rather than the myriad cultural identities in our collective diversity. My focus on culture, language, gender, class, and religion is anthropologically based, not race based. Conflating culture and race is a common misinterpretation among some individuals who work with diverse groups of students. CLR makes clear the distinction and fosters understanding of the need to avoid such identity confusion.

2. I use CLR in order to emphasize the language aspect of culture. I believe that there is nothing more cultural about us as humans than the use of our home language. Linguistic identity is a crucial aspect of who we are. By itself, the term *culture* subsumes language; consequently, linguistic identity is obscured. By adding language to the overall term, the intentionality of the linguistic focus is demonstrated equally to what we stereotypically think about culture. In short, we are what we speak and, to a large extent, our language is a representation of our heritage, including family, community, and history.

3. CLR speaks to the specific use of pedagogy versus teaching and learning. Pedagogy is a five-star word frequently thrown around in academic circles with the result that some people consider the term to be jargon. I consider pedagogy to be a powerful term in its meaning and its functionality in CLR. Meriam-Webster's (2011) online dictionary defines pedagogy as the method and practice of teaching, especially as an academic subject or theoretical concept. I define *pedagogy* as the how and why of teaching, the strategic use of methods, and the rationale behind why instructional decisions are made. Pedagogy is usually the most often-missed facet of culturally responsive

teaching. Without the pedagogy, there is only theory on how to respond to students' cultural and linguistic needs, and theory alone does not adequately serve teachers and students.

To sum up, what a concept is called matters. In society, how we label something speaks to what it means to us symbolically. *Culturally and linguistically responsive pedagogy* is the concept that is developed in this book.

Defining Culturally and Linguistically Responsive Pedagogy

Pause to Ponder

- Are you familiar with the term *culturally and linguistically responsive pedagogy*?

- Where have you encountered it?

- How do you define it?

- What sources have informed your definition?

Most proponents of culturally relevant teaching will point to *The Dreamkeepers*, Gloria Ladson-Billings's (1994) groundbreaking book, as the star in the culturally responsive universe. This work has defined what many have come to know about the approach, and her description of six culturally relevant teachers is a must-read for those interested in being culturally responsive. She provides a classic definition of *culturally responsive teaching*: "A pedagogy that empowers students intellectually, socially, emotionally, and politically by using cultural and historical referents to convey knowledge, to impart skills, and to change attitudes" (Ladson-Billings 1994, 13). Teachers practicing culturally relevant teaching know how to support student learning by consciously creating social interactions that help them meet the criteria of academic success, cultural competence, and critical consciousness. In addition to the work of Ladson-Billings, advanced students of culturally responsive teaching will point to the contributions of Ramirez and Castaneda (1974). Many cite this reference as the earliest introduction of culturally responsive teaching, showing that the concept itself goes back many years. While Ramirez and Castaneda may have introduced culturally responsive teaching to the research, Ladson-Billings put it on the national map.

Geneva Gay's text, *Culturally Responsive Teaching: Theory, Research, and Practice* (2000), is by most accounts the second-most influential work on culturally responsive teaching. She added pedagogy to the concept and became the leader in the second wave of books and articles that would build upon Ladson-Billings' work. She defines culturally responsive pedagogy as "the use of cultural knowledge, prior experiences, frames of reference, and performance styles of ethnically diverse students to make learning encounters more relevant to, and effective for, them" (Gay 2000, 31). This pedagogy teaches *to and through* the strengths of these students. It is culturally validating and affirming. In addition to the focus on pedagogy, Gay provides positive achievement data supporting the work from districts and schools across the nation. This addition of results data was important to establish the credibility of culturally responsive teaching, which had been an easy target for critics of the approach. Unfortunately, some criticism can still be found today. Goodwin (2008) cites that there is no research that supports culturally responsive teaching correlated to student achievement. But this statement is based on research from the 1970s and does not account for the evolution of the theory since that time, not to mention any recent research. Other researchers who have made important contributions to the literature of culturally responsive teaching include Lisa Delpit and

Culturally and Linguistically Responsive Pedagogy (CLR) is the validation and affirmation of the home (indigenous) culture and home language for the purposes of building and bridging the student to success in the culture of academia and mainstream society.

J. K. E. Dowdy (2002), Etta Hollins (2008), Jacqueline Irvine (1991), and Villegas and Lucas (2007). These researchers agree on a key element of culturally responsive teaching: it responds to students' needs by taking into account cultural and linguistic factors in their worlds.

This definition of CLR is central to the content of this book as well as to the work I do with educators around the country. Specifically, CLR is going to where the students are culturally and linguistically, for the aim of bringing them where they need to be academically. Metaphorically, CLR is the opposite of the sink-or-swim approach to teaching and learning in traditional schools. CLR means that teachers jump into the pool with the learners, guide them with appropriate instruction, scaffold as necessary, and provide for independence when they are ready. *Validation* is the intentional and purposeful legitimatization of the home culture and language of the student. Such validation has been traditionally delegitimatized by historical institutional and structural racism, stereotypes, and generalizations primarily carried forth through mainstream media. *Affirmation* is the intentional and purposeful effort to reverse the negative stereotypes of nonmainstream cultures and languages portrayed in historical perspective.

This definition of CLR is meant to be broad, covering a range of cultural identities and languages. It centers on ethnic identity in the cultural context and on nonstandard languages in the linguistic context. But in no way is the definition exclusive to any one group. Later in the chapter, I distinguish the different identities that comprise who we are as humans and the cultures that come with those identities.

Benefits of Culturally and Linguistically Responsive Pedagogy

The simple answer to the question of who benefits from culturally and linguistically responsive pedagogy is *all students*. A more specific answer delves into who these students are most likely to be in the sense of culture, not race, in the classroom. A survey of any past or recent standardized data gives the answer of who is and who is not achieving in our schools. In the context of academic failure and behavior issues, CLR best benefits *any* student who is identified as *underserved* as opposed to the more commonly labeled *underachieving* or *underperforming* student.

According to my definition below, the school as an institution is failing the student. Granted, the breadth of the definition speaks to the simplicity of who can be served by CLR. At face value, *underserved* includes many students. If teachers think about the underserved students in their particular context, they are probably thinking of students of different races, cultures, and languages, or special education and even gifted students. Underserved encompasses those students who are receiving bad customer service from the school, similar to you or me not receiving the best service in a restaurant or a department store. The difference is that we can request to see a manager or even walk out of the establishment. Students cannot! They are stuck in a situation where the institution is failing them, so instead of asking for the manager, they simply check out mentally and emotionally. Or even worse, far too many are pushed out of school and become what are commonly known as *dropouts*.

An **underserved student** is any student who is not successful academically, socially, and/or behaviorally in school because the school as an institution is not being responsive to that student's needs.

Pause to Ponder

- Who are the underserved students in your district or your school?

- Why are they underserved?

- What are their needs?

- What is your district or school doing as an institution to address the needs of these students?

Looking more specifically at which group of students is likely to be underserved reveals why CLR is really important and shows the complexity involved in implementing the approach. Pretend that we asked all the underserved students you identified to come to the gymnasium. The research (Goodwin 2008) tells us who these students are most likely to be: African Americans, Mexican Americans (as opposed to the over-generalized term *Latino*), Native Americans, Samoan Americans and/or Eastern Asian immigrants and Asian Americans. Keep in mind that the overall intention is to better serve all students, but when we look at who is in the gymnasium now, we find these to be primarily students of color. The students are like those dissatisfied customers in a department store who need to be better served simply because of their place in the gymnasium and not endemically because of their race, nationality, ethnicity, or language. Bluntly put, we serve them because they are in the gymnasium of the underserved, not because of who they are racially, ethnically, or otherwise. In order to fully understand why students of color in particular are in the room, we need to examine the sociohistorical, sociopolitical, and sociolinguistic contexts.

Sociohistorical Context

The capstone research of John Ogbu (1978) indicates that many of these students can be described as involuntary immigrants to America. Ogbu posited that the experience in the American school was very different for an involuntary immigrant when compared to that of a voluntary immigrant or the Ellis Island immigrants. Involuntary immigrants, historically speaking, are more likely to be found in the so-called achievement gap and less likely to have post-secondary opportunities that then lead to economic success. Voluntary immigrants, on the other hand, tend to perform well academically and find post-secondary opportunities that lead to economic viability and stability. The significant difference is that the involuntary immigrant's move to America comes through colonization, enslavement, conquest, or less than legal means. Simply put, these immigrants did not come through Ellis Island.

Whereas the path to success in the American school for the voluntary immigrant has come through a process of successful assimilation, the path for the involuntary immigrant has been more a process of forced or unsuccessful assimilation. The relevance of assimilation cannot be emphasized enough. In order to attain the American dream, most immigrants will have to assimilate into mainstream culture. The formula for success in academia and mainstream culture is straightforward. When given the choice of assimilating from one's indigenous (home) culture and language into that of the mainstream culture, many ethnic groups had great success in pursuing and achieving the American dream. On the contrary, those ethnic groups that were forced into the mainstream culture did not have a choice. Consequently, they did not have access to the tools that would have enabled them to become part of mainstream society. For example, the long-lasting effects of slavery, legal segregation, and institutional racism on the education of Africans in America have been well documented, and these factors still resonate in the schools today (Anderson 1995; Smith 1998; Williams 1990). Over 30 years ago, Ogbu (1978, 91) said, "Before 1960 most societies did not provide their minorities with equal educational opportunities." Howard (1988) professes that of the innumerable rights African Americans were denied during slavery, none were more important than education. The same can be said for many of the involuntary immigrant groups. According to Javier San Roman, former student advocate at our laboratory school and now a consultant with me in the national work for Mexican-American students, the introduction to compulsory public education began with the inferior segregated Mexican schools that operated throughout the Southwestern United States. Often the rationale given for segregation of non-Black students at this time was that Mexican children posed potential health risks or were not redeemable outside of providing a basic level of education that was designed to prepare them for low-wage manual labor. Notable school desegregation court cases such as *Roberto Alvarez v. Lemon Grove School District* in 1931 (the country's first successful school desegregation court victory) and *Mendez et al. v. Westminster* in 1947 dealt a significant blow to the rationale behind school segregation for all students.

For the Native American and Hawaiian students, the process of the introduction to public education was carried forth through the boarding schools and academies that were designed to save the "native" and kill the "savage." At the Indian boarding schools, students were deliberately alienated from their language and culture and taught to value the alleged superiority of European culture and language. The early experiences of Native Hawaiian students mirrored the devaluation of their cultural and linguistic heritage in favor of European models. The collective experience of all involuntary immigrants in public education has been one of institutional neglect and a pervasive and pernicious deficit oriented towards the cultural and linguistic differences that they bring to the classroom.

Sociopolitical Context

The systematic denial of indigenous culture and language for involuntary immigrants was utilized as a means to eliminate their culture and linguistic heritages. These populations were in effect institutionally denied their own culture and at the same time were not given the opportunity to become part of the mainstream culture. Joel Spring (1994) calls this process *deculturalization*. He defines deculturalization as the "educational process of destroying a people's culture and replacing it with a new culture. It is one of the most inhumane acts one can partake in. Culture shapes a person's beliefs, values, and morals. In the United States, historically the education system deculturalized the cultures of Native Americans; African Americans, Mexican Americans; Puerto Ricans; and immigrants from Ireland, Southern and Eastern Europe, and Asia" (1994, 7). Providing further evidence referring to Native Americans, Spring notes, "Missionaries wanted to develop written Native American Languages not as a means of preserving Native American history and religions, but so they could translate religious tracts to teach protestant Anglo-Saxon culture. In contrast, Sequoyah development of a written Cherokee language was for the purpose of preserving Cherokee culture" (1994, 28).

Angela Valenzuela (1999) terms this process of eliminating one's home culture as *subtractive schooling*. Subtractive schooling is the divestment of students of important social and cultural resources, leaving them progressively vulnerable to academic failure, and the discouragement of cultural identity by presenting such characteristics as undesirable. Valenzuela says of the Mexican American student, "I came to locate 'the problem' of achievement squarely in school-based relationships and organizational structures and policies designed to erase students' culture. Over the three years in which I collected and analyzed my data, I became increasingly convinced that schooling is organized in ways that subtract resources from Mexican youth" (1999, 10). Part of being culturally and linguistically responsive requires the intentional effort to combat the long-lasting effects of deculturalization through validation and affirmation of the home language and culture. To effectively implement CLR, educators must recognize and understand the cultural and linguistic behaviors that need to be legitimized and made positive.

Another commonality among students who are most likely to be underserved is their use of a nonstandard language as their home language. Historically, generations of these students' forefathers and foremothers who were in this country were involuntarily denied quality formal second-language opportunities. In specific cases, as with the enslaved Africans, people were told that if they spoke their native language, their tongues would be cut out; if they congregated with more than two, they would be beaten; and if they were caught trying to learn the language of the land, they would be punished or even killed. Here is an example of an enslavement code, written essentially as law and more commonly known as the *Black Codes* or *Slave Codes*:

> Punishment for teaching slaves or free persons of color to read:

> If any slave, Negro, or free person of color, or any white person, shall teach any other slave, Negro, or free person of color, to read or write either written or printed characters, the said free person of color or slave shall be punished by fine and whipping, or fine or whipping, at the discretion of the court (http://academic.udayton.edu/race/02rights/slavelaw.htm#11.)

Similarly, a persistent cultural myth about Mexican American students is that they value labor over education and often drop out of school because they are not interested in education. In fact, it is structural economic pressure and depressed wages for Mexican American workers that often burden youth to attend to immediate short-term needs. Once again, this would be a consequence of overgeneralizing a socioeconomic behavior to an ethnocultural behavior.

Ethnolinguists have explained that under these constraints, a second language formed that was a combination of the deep structure of the first or indigenous language and the vocabulary of the dominating language. In America, the dominant language would be Standard English, or Mainstream English. Linguists, in general, have labeled these second languages *nonstandard*. These languages have remained intact across generations to present day. For African American students, the nonstandard language is known most commonly as African American Vernacular English, or AAVE. For Native Americans, there are numerous Native American dialects. Looking at the Mexican American, particularly second or third generation, the nonstandard language is called *Chicano English* (Fought 2003). Lastly, Hawaiian Americans speak what is known as Hawaiian Pidgin English, or HPE. The linguistic characteristics of these nonstandard languages are described in Chapter 6.

In the context of CLR, the key is to understand that these populations share this sociolinguistic history. They share the history of nonstandard languages among racially isolated descendants who were denied the use of their indigenous language and have traditionally performed poorly in schools (Baugh 2004). As with the cultural behaviors noted earlier, in many cases, the linguistic behaviors of these students are viewed as signs of a deficiency, laziness, or other aberration. In order to be linguistically responsive to the students in the classroom, such behaviors, therefore, have to be legitimized and made positive.

The Purpose of Culturally and Linguistically Responsive Pedagogy

Given the historical context for who benefits most from culturally and linguistically responsive pedagogy, it is easier to understand why we need CLR. Inject the topics of race, culture, and language into almost any conversation, and you are very likely to find an intense and provocative discussion. Enter those same topics in a discussion among educators, and you encounter a surly tension with a tempered vibe. When the topics of race, culture, and language are coupled with the pressure of increasing standardized test scores, educators are faced with simple but complex choices of how to address the real issues of diversity and improving student achievement.

The simplicity of the choices is often provided through state, federal, and district curricular mandates with quick fix-it programs that ultimately do not address the diversity issues with substantive and sustaining change. Such mandates invariably replicate the persistent stagnation and failure of the school as an institution to meet the needs of underserved students. The difficulty of making appropriate choices is either masked in the negative beliefs, attitudes, and expectations about certain students, or is clouded by the desire and the intention to make changes, but without the knowledge of how to do so instructionally. Culturally and linguistically responsive pedagogy deals with the complexity of both these negative mindsets and the well-intentioned desires to make changes that will matter.

Eliminating the Deficit Perspective

When it comes to consideration of the culture and language of the populations that have been identified here, many educators' beliefs, attitudes, and mindsets are deficit oriented. In essence, this means that the students are blamed for their failures and are seen as the problem. The view of an educator with a deficit mindset is reflected in such observations as these:

- If we had better students, then we would have better schools.

- Our scores were good until *they* started coming here.

- Everyone in our school seems to be doing well except for *those* kids.

- The students are myopically viewed as lacking *something*.

Culturally and linguistically, the underserved students are all too frequently seen as deficient, deviant, defiant, disruptive, and disrespectful. What they bring to the classroom culturally and linguistically is not seen as an asset, but as a liability.

The first purpose of CLR is to refute deficit thinking by having educators undergo a change in heart and in mind about these students. I call this change a *mindset shift*, or as my colleague and former CLAS teacher Kiechelle Russell dubbed it, a "mindshift." In order to be culturally and linguistically responsive, educators have to shift their beliefs, attitudes, and knowledge to a stance that sees what the student brings culturally and linguistically as an asset, a capability, and an element that can be built upon. In this mindshift, students are not the problem but rather the source of the solution.

A second purpose for CLR pedagogy is to clarify what is meant specifically by culture while simultaneously giving educators an awareness of some of the noted cultural and linguistic behaviors of underserved student populations. What lingers is a confusion between race and culture and the various identities that comprise who we are culturally. We are made up of at least seven separate identities, of which all but one have an unrelated cultural connection. The seven identities are race, gender, nationality, religion, ethnicity, class, and age.

These identities examined in isolation say something about who we are and why we enact certain behaviors, or make what I call *cultural determinations*. The exception is race. In other words, our behaviors are culturally determined by these identities only. But race determines nothing about our behavior. For example, there are some behaviors that we do simply based on how old we are or what decade we grew up in and nothing else. Some decisions and behaviors are based on our socioeconomic identity and nothing else. Before examining other examples, I want to clearly eliminate racial identity as the one factor that has nothing to do with cultural determination.

Our racial identity is very clear: it is the biological DNA representation that gives us our blood lineage and, for example what diseases we may be prone to (good information to know). Other than that, racial identity really tells us nothing about who we are as individuals. The salient point is that racial identity has nothing to do with our cultural identity. Racial identity does not necessitate or affect any of our other identities—age, religion, gender, or nationality. There is nothing that we do racially that is connected to who we are mentally or behaviorally. Although we are locked into our racial identity by birth and perhaps genomes, we remain free to be who we are ethnically or otherwise.

> In the context of culturally and linguistically responsiveness, **culture** means a behavior learned from the home or the community that is passed down from generation to generation and represents our heritage.

On the other hand, by acknowledging our various cultural identities in explicit terms, we are acknowledging a cultural complexity that truly speaks to the kaleidoscope that has been guised under the narrowness of racial identity and the thickness of racism for too long. From an ethnocultural perspective, being African American does not mean that one is Black, if Black is seen as an ethnic identity no different from Irish, Armenian, or Jewish. Being Caucasian American does not mean that one is White Anglo-Saxon Protestant or Catholic ethnically. Villegas and Lucas (2007) define culture as the way life organized within an identifiable community or group. This includes the ways that a community uses language, interacts with one another, takes turns to talk, relates to time and space, and approaches learning. The group patterns that exist reflect the standards or norms used by community members to make sense of the world. Simply, cultural identity is the way we see the world.

Culture or ethnic identity differs from race, nationality, and socioeconomic identity in that our ethnocultural identity is passed down from generation to generation. What is most confusing is that sometimes who we are ethnoculturally can be mistaken for our national cultural identity and/or our socioeconomic cultural identity. In these cases, there are behaviors that we exhibit based simply on our nationality or our economic status. Consider the two questions that follow:

- Why do you celebrate the Fourth of July if you are a United States citizen?

- Where do you wash your clothes?

Before answering the first question, though, ask yourself if you celebrate the Fourth of July because you are White Anglo-Saxon or Latino (ethnically and not racially speaking) or because you are a citizen of the United States. For the second question, by knowing where you wash your clothes, I can, most of the time, accurately guess your economic status. If you regularly wash your clothes in a laundromat, wash house, or building complex, my guess would be you are of a lower or working socioeconomic class. If you wash your clothes in your home, then my guess would be middle class. If someone washes your clothes for you, then you might be upper class. The point is that the Independence Day that you celebrate is determined not by your ethnocultural identity but by your national cultural identity. The way you wash your clothes is not determined by your Black or White ethnicity but by your economic identity.

The central feature of CLR is the ethnocultural identity of the students, but not to the exclusion of the other identities that come with culture. Additionally, educators have to be responsive to gender culture, national culture, socioeconomic culture, and youth culture—or what I call the *rings of culture*.

Figure 1.1 illustrates the rings of culture. Each of these rings is a potential source of responsiveness for the educator. Notice that race does not appear in the figure.

Fig. 1.1 Rings of Culture

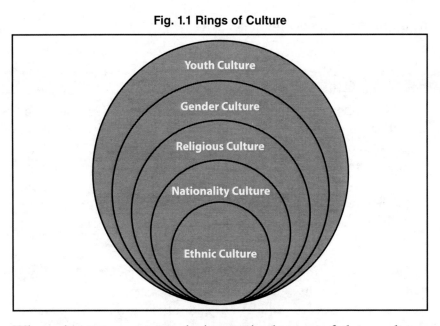

What educators must not do is to mistake one of these cultures for another, and they certainly should not confuse any of these with race, which often happens in the classroom. Such mistakes affect the dynamics of instruction. Sometimes, educators will make judgments about African American students' behaviors as being Black ethnically when in actuality the behaviors are more in alignment with lower socioeconomic behaviors. For example, consider the familiar stereotype about some African American or Black students being unlikely to do their homework. Educators who make these assumptions about Black students overgeneralize a socioeconomic behavior, in this case doing homework, to an ethnocultural behavior. Indeed, the fact that some educators would conclude that Black students are less likely to do the homework causes these educators to miss the opportunity to be responsive to the economic culture. Similarly, a persistent cultural myth about Mexican American students is that they value labor over education and often drop out of school because they are not interested in education. In fact, it is often structural economic pressure and depressed wages for Mexican American workers that often burden youth to attend to immediate short-term needs. Once again, this would be a consequence of overgeneralizing a socioeconomic behavior to an ethnocultural behavior.

Promoting Validation and Affirmation

Another important aspect of the CLR focus on ethnocultural identity is the validation and affirmation that is associated with responsiveness. Recall that part of the meaning of CLR is to make culturally and linguistically legitimate and positive that which has been made illegitimate and negative by the institution and mainstream media. It is the ethnocultural identity that needs to be most validated and affirmed. The issue for educators is to appropriately identify those ethnocultural behaviors.

Based on the definition, the ethnocultural behaviors of the most underserved students can be pinpointed, measured, and understood for the purposes of validation and affirmation. In general, these behaviors include preferences for variation and spontaneity, sociocentricity, high-movement contexts, approximation of time, collaboration, inductive reasoning, verbal overlap, and pragmatic, interpersonal, and affective language use. These cultural behaviors, which are typically seen as negative in the culture of school, are the ones that are to be validated and affirmed in comparison to the general behaviors of the school and mainstream culture. In contrast, the expected cultural behaviors of the school and mainstream culture include a focus on prompting, independence, low-movement contexts, competition, deductive reasoning, and verbal communication. Once educators have validated and affirmed the students' home cultural norms and mores, they can then begin practicing CLR notably by building awareness of and bridging toward the cultural norms and mores of the school and mainstream culture.

Ethnocultural behaviors are defined as characteristics of cognitive, affective, and physiological behaviors that serve as relatively stable indicators of how learners perceive, interact with, and respond to the learning environment.

Focus on Linguistic Behaviors

Similarly, the linguistic behaviors of the students have to be validated and affirmed in the context of their home language for the purposes of building and bridging to proficiency in Standard English and Academic Language. In order to be linguistically responsive, educators have to subscribe to the following three linguistic absolutes:

1. All language is good for the communicative purposes it serves. There is no such thing as proper English, bad English, street speech, or "gutter talk" in the context of interpersonal communication.

2. All linguistic forms are rule governed and systematic and are not randomly formed or put together haphazardly. They are regular in their phonological and syntactic patterns.

3. As infants and toddlers, beginning as early as prebirth, we learn the language that is spoken in the home by the primary caregivers.

Understanding these three linguistic principles allows for an open-minded discussion around nonstandard languages.

In general, the issue of the use of nonstandard linguistic forms extends beyond the United States. Corson (1997) reveals that formal educational policies for the treatment of nonstandard varieties are conspicuous by their absence in most educational systems. He points out that these varieties are nonetheless brought into the work of the school in one way or another. Educators have to recognize that children coming from these backgrounds often possess two or more linguistic varieties—one of which they use in their home and community and the other in the school. Still other forms may exist. The bottom line is that students speaking nonstandard language varieties are frequently penalized for using language that is different from the linguistic capital that has high status in the school.

Corson (1997) chronicles how the history of prejudice against the users of nonstandard varieties of a dominant language probably can be traced to the Ancient Greeks. Evidence shows that the use of different Greek dialects was used as a way of stereotyping other Greeks. A Roman playwright, Publilius Syrus, wrote that "speech is a mirror to the soul; as a man speaks, so is he" (Syrus). In France, the purpose of the Academie Francaise was to maintain the purity of the French standard variety. A national policy such as this has a direct impact on schooling for French children. Similarly, in Spain and Portugal, the standard varieties are elevated. Sometimes, negative consequences affect those speakers of nonstandard varieties.

In the United States, William Labov's studies (1972) of Black American and Puerto Rican vernaculars of English have proven to be groundbreaking. He found that people from different sociocultural backgrounds speak different kinds of English that in important respects deviate systematically and regularly from one another. These findings helped to overturn the common stereotype that these and many other varieties of language are incorrect forms of English. Labov's legacy has been the evidence that nonstandard language varieties have their particular norms and rules of use. Therefore, these language forms deserve respect and valuation. However, the institution of education itself as a standard and routine practice devalues varieties that are very different from the dominant form.

The nonstandard languages that become the focus of applying linguistically responsive pedagogy are tied to the specific populations described here. These languages are Hawaiian Pidgin English (HPE), Chicano English (CE), Native American dialects, and African American Vernacular English (AAVE). Each of these linguistic entities has its rule-governed system. Inclusive of all the language dimensions, examples of specific features of these languages are provided in Chapter 6.

Labov (1972) has argued that there is no real basis for attributing poor performance to the grammatical and phonological characteristics of any nonstandard variety of English. He found that not the African American Vernacular English itself but teachers' low expectations that were based on linguistic misperceptions were the culprit of academic failure. The students were deemed deficient because their language variety was wrongly judged in the context of school language. Generally speaking, educational policy for the use of nonstandard language forms is limited mainly because of simple ignorance about the range of varieties that can and do coexist in a single linguistic space (Corson 1997).

When educators recognize students' linguistic behaviors or the use of the rules of home languages as positives and not deficits, they can then begin to validate and to affirm the students' language. Consequently, teachers can begin the process of building and bridging that will enable students to function within the language of school.

Situational appropriateness is the concept of determining what cultural or linguistic behavior is most appropriate for the situation. In other words, students are allowed to make choices around cultural and linguistic behaviors dependent on the situation but without giving up or sacrificing what they consider to be their base culture or language. Situational appropriateness is the crux of CLR. Understanding the concept will enable you to comprehend the pedagogical underpinnings or, more to the point, enrich the instructional experience for your students as well as yourself. Related to situational appropriateness is the action of *codeswitching*, or what I call cultureswitching.

Codeswitching means the act of switching from one cultural or linguistic behavior to another for the purpose of being situationally appropriate.

Situational Appropriateness

The processes of validating, affirming, building, and bridging are moving the student toward being situationally appropriate.

Note that in the linguistic literature, codeswitching has a very different meaning from that which applies in CLR. In linguistics, the term is usually associated with an action whereby one language is being utilized along with an infusion of the vocabulary of another language into the first language being spoken or written (Gardner-Chloros 2009). Codeswitching in CLR is used more literally and does not carry the pejorative association that is sometimes attached to the term. In the context of CLR, codeswitching is an intentional choice to shift from one linguistic or cultural mode into another one skillfully and proficiently without giving up, disavowing, or abandoning the home culture or language. If students who have been traditionally underserved are to overcome the barriers to achieving success in the school and mainstream cultures, they must master the concept of situational appropriateness and the act of codeswitching—culturally and linguistically. Situational appropriateness and codeswitching provide the necessary instructional experiences that form culturally and linguistically responsive pedagogy. Implementing CLR pedagogy is the focus of the remaining chapters in this book. Each chapter describes activities that enable teachers to use CLR pedagogy consistently in their classrooms.

Summary

In order for educators to be focused and to improve instruction for underserved students, a single term and definition of *culturally responsive teaching* must be adopted. The term I prescribe is *culturally and linguistically responsive teaching and learning*, or CLR. Four features define the key aspects of CLR: *validation*, *affirmation*, *build*, and *bridge*. CLR benefits all students but is most powerful with students who are underserved. To *validate* and to *affirm* means understanding the complexity of culture and the many forms it takes, including age, gender, and social class. This understanding creates opportunities for meaning making experiences in school. Likewise, acknowledging and affirming the home language of the student as a nonstandard language speaker is another opportunity for validation and affirmation. In both cases, the general purpose is to set the framework for teaching the students to be able to adjust their language and behavior as necessary to be situationally appropriate.

Reflection Guide

Think back to your responses to the statements in the Anticipation Guide at the beginning of this chapter. Have your responses changed? Which parts of the chapter did you find most helpful in clarifying your understanding of culturally responsive teaching?

_____ Culturally responsive teaching is meant to help with race relations among educators and students.

_____ All students can achieve highly when given the opportunity to learn.

_____ Racial identity and cultural identity are synonymous.

_____ Nonstandard English is a simplified version of Standard English.

_____ Socioeconomic status is the most critical factor in student success.

1. From your reading of this chapter, what advice will you offer your school leadership about ways in which to improve instruction for underserved students?

2. In what ways are your instructional purposes consistent with those of CLR pedagogy? To what extent are you successful in meeting instructional purposes for underserved students in your classes?

3. Which ideas in this chapter have you found to be most meaningful for your teaching situation? Share your observations with colleagues.

The Pedagogy of Cultural and Linguistical Responsiveness

Chapter 2

Anticipation Guide

What thoughts came to mind when you read the title of this chapter?

Do you agree or disagree with the following statements about the pedagogy of cultural and linguistic responsiveness?

 Culturally and linguistically responsive pedagogy is a curriculum.

_____ In using CLR, I should abandon what I have known to be successful with students.

_____ CLR strategies and activities can be infused into broad instructional areas.

_____ All the activities or strategies must *always* be culturally or linguistically responsive.

Moving from Theory to Practice

If you were to take all the books, research articles, and presentations on culturally relevant teaching and put them in one area, you could probably fill up an average-size hotel room from the floor to the ceiling. If you were then to take all the books, research articles, and presentations on the classroom practices for culturally relevant teaching, you would be lucky to fill up the bathroom. The literature on the theory of CLR far outpaces the research on the instructional practice. Because of the lack of information on actual practice, the approach overall has suffered. CLR has remained too abstract for some practitioners who view it as a good idea in concept but not realistic for use in the classroom. For others, CLR is not sufficiently results based, difficult to construct in the classroom context, and not student focused. Guaranteed attacks on CLR come in the form of questions about achievement data and exemplary classroom models.

A great part of my inspiration to become engaged in the study of CLR was to defend it against such attacks. Initially, I observed that some attacks were warranted, particularly in the lack of exemplary classroom models. However, I thought that the best way to address such criticisms was to create a school centered on the concept of culturally and linguistically responsive pedagogy. Consequently, I, along with two colleagues, Janis Bucknor and Anthony Jackson, and a team of outstanding teachers started the Culture and Language Academy of Success (CLAS), a nonaffiliated kindergarten-through-eighth-grade charter school in Los Angeles. Centered on a positive mindset about students' culture and language, CLAS has become one of the few models in the nation to demonstrate what CLR looks like in practice and in which instruction has been transformed by the use of strategies and the activities prescribed by the approach. The positive impact of CLR pedagogy is revealed in the school's test results. According to the California Standards Test and the Academic Performance Index, CLAS has maintained high achievement results specifically in English/Language Arts when compared to the local district and the state. The Academic Performance Index (API), the California state report card on schools, shows that for 2010, CLAS has a score of 822 in its elementary school and 728 for the middle school. Figure 2.1 shows a comparison between CLAS and the Los Angeles Unified School District over five years. Similarly, according to the Federal Annual Yearly Progress (AYP) report card, nearly 60 percent of CLAS students are advanced or proficient in reading/english language arts. These impressive results serve to inform those who have criticized the value and effectiveness of CLR pedagogy.

Fig. 2.1 Academic Performance Index (API) Comparison of CLAS and LAUSD from 2005–2010

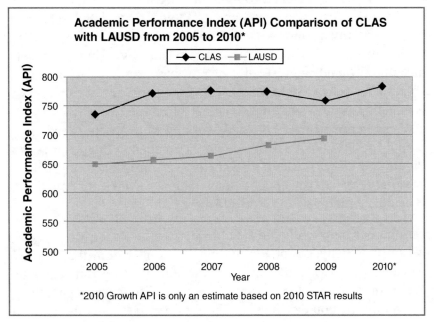

The Story of the Culture and Language Academy of Success (CLAS)

CLAS was born out of a need and a vision. Understanding the need was simple: Los Angeles Unified School District as an institution, like many other districts across the country, was and is in need of closing the so-called achievement gap, particularly with African American students. Despite countless attempts in the form of programs, forums, and initiatives, little progress was being made. The vision grew out of frustration for a group of educators working with a program originally known as the Language Development Program of African American Students (LDPAAS). Directed by Noma LeMoine, nationally renowned expert and my mentor, LDPAAS focused on increasing student achievement for African American students by using the tenets of culturally and linguistically responsive teaching. As program coordinator for Dr. LeMoine, I was responsible for designing and conducting professional development programs, writing curricula and instructional materials, and working with teacher leaders at school sites. LDPAAS evolved into the Academic English Mastery Program (AEMP) where the focus was broadened to include a variety of student populations, namely Mexican American, Hawaiian American, and Native American.

Despite our hard work and satellite success in the AEMP schools, we invariably hit the proverbial glass ceiling within the LAUSD bureaucracy. Collectively, we knew that if given an authentic opportunity without the constraints of the traditional, though failing, institution, we could develop a schoolwide model for culturally and linguistically responsive teaching. At the time, between 2002 and 2003, the best avenue for change was through development of a charter school, which was then (as opposed to now) a politically viable means for an alternative school. Together Janis Bucknor, Anthony Jackson, and I wrote a proposal for a charter school start-up grant to the California Department of Education. We were awarded the grant, and CLAS was opened in the fall of 2003 with 140 students and six classrooms. As of fall 2010, we have grown to over 300 students and 15 classrooms. CLAS is the living embodiment of a schoolwide model of culturally and linguistically responsive teaching and learning. A visitor can go into any classroom and see culturally and linguistically responsive teaching at work. CLAS is a laboratory school where we experiment with instructional innovations, differentiated instruction, classroom management, and other school-related topics. For the past nine years, CLAS has stood out as one of the very few, if only, nationwide models of CLR.

What Is the CLR Formula?

The cultural and linguistic pedagogy that CLAS as well as many other classrooms around the country employs, is based on an instructional formula that any teacher can use after gaining a foundational understanding of the theory. The CLR formula has the following three parts, all of which are necessary for successful implementation of the pedagogy:

Culturally and linguistically responsive pedagogy is not a curriculum and does not come in a box. It is an approach—a way of thinking about how to instruct and how to create an instructional experience for the students that validates, affirms, illuminates, inspires, and motivates them.

Pause to Ponder

- What does the term *pedagogical area* suggest to you?

- In what ways do you think pedagogical areas should be designed to meet the needs of underserved students?

Pedagogy is defined as the how and why of teaching. Many administrators can attest to the fact that they have teachers who are strong in the how of teaching but weak in the content, or they have teachers strong in content but weak in the methodology. Strong pedagogy speaks to finding a balance between the how and what of teaching—that is, combining appropriate methodology with knowledge of the content. CLR relies upon this pedagogical balance. In order to be successful in CLR, the practitioner has to understand the balance of the how and the what.

The how of methodology comes in two parts: strategy and activity. *Strategy* means that the instructional activities must be strategically and deliberately determined. Teachers must weigh several factors, including outcome, purpose, standards-based relation, time allocation, resources, students' background knowledge, environmental space, assessment methods, and a host of other variables. Considerations of these factors will in effect determine the strategy or the activity to be used. The *activity* selected puts the strategy to action, and a wide range of activities can be chosen. Many of the activities used in CLR are familiar to teachers, but the difference lies in the strategic use of the activities to further responsiveness to the cultural and linguistic needs of the students. Many participants in my professional development programs have commented on how they have previously used the activities. What is new to them is application in the context of a strategy or in the context of CLR. The difference between a strategy and an activity can be summed up metaphorically in how we play chess. Skilled players come to the match with a strategy in mind, a game plan, and a pattern of attack. The players then carry out a plan through movement of either the players or activities. Similar to a chess game, CLR involves having a game plan and a series of moves designed to implement that plan.

I have identified five broad pedagogical areas that can be infused with CLR strategies and activities. These areas are:

- Responsive Classroom Management

- Responsive Academic Literacy (or use of text)

- Responsive Academic Vocabulary

- Responsive Academic Language (or situational appropriateness)

- Responsive Learning Environment

These pedagogical areas represent the general categories that I believe that all classrooms—regardless of grade level or content area—should have in place effectively and efficiently. In my discussion of CLR pedagogy, I include the term *responsive* in the label for each category to ensure that instruction centers on culturally and linguistically appropriate activities. These categories are the basis for instructional failure or success. CLR does not replace or shield ineffective instruction. At times, administrators will send so-called "bad" or ineffective teachers to our trainings, thinking that these teachers can be turned into "good" teachers through CLR. This is asking too much of the approach. CLR can make a difference for many inadequacies in instruction, but when the fundamentals are not effectively in place, using CLR is like putting a new suit on a dirty body. To be most effective with CLR, we have to make sure the body is clean first, meaning that educators should make sure the fundamentals are effectively in place.

Within each pedagogical area are subcategories that depict specific foci for the instruction in that area. These subcategories specify aspects for the teacher to consider when strategically determining how to do various activities. Figure 2.2 illustrates aspects of four general pedagogical areas: responsive classroom management, responsive academic literacy, responsive academic vocabulary, responsive academic language, and the subcategories of activities within each.

Fig. 2.2 Infusing CLR into Four Educational Pedagogies

Responsive Classroom Management	Responsive Academic Literacy	Responsive Academic Vocabulary	Responsive Academic Language
• Ways for responding • Ways for discussing • Attention signals • Movement	• Read-aloud storytelling • Supplemental text selections • Interaction with text strategies	• Focus on common strategies • Building on students' words (personal thesaurus) • Focus on low-frequency words (personal dictionary)	• Contrastive analysis • Revision process • Role playing

Responsive Classroom Management

No one can argue against the need for an effectively managed classroom (Marzano 2009). Students need to learn in a safe, secure, and positive environment that is conducive to learning and enables them to function optimally. Under the pedagogical area of classroom management, there are four subcategories: ways for responding, ways for discussing, attention signals, and movement. On the whole, these subcategories represent what *all* classrooms should have in place. Every classroom should have effective and efficient ways of having students respond to questions and prompts and discuss topics. Every classroom should have effective and efficient attention signals to indicate when the teacher needs to bring everyone back after conducting a discussion in groups.

Furthermore, classroom activities should be designed to enable students to move around the room to provide opportunities for interactions with several classmates for a variety of purposes.

Responsive Academic Literacy

Responsive use of fiction and nonfiction text is necessary to enhance students' success within the content areas. Strong literacy skills—reading, writing, speaking, and listening—are central to success in most content areas. Students who are strong readers and writers also tend to be strong in mathematics, science, and social studies (Krashen 2004). Think about it. Have you ever seen a student who is in both a basic reading class and in an Algebra 2 class? The answer is generally no. The effective use of literacy is a very important area for infusing CLR pedagogy. Reading aloud as a form of storytelling provides a cultural base for the students in a classroom where CLR is implemented. Supplemental resources can be used to augment the core texts within the subject areas. For example, a science teacher can include supplemental articles, stories, and facts relevant to the standards-based topics from the mandated book that the students are required to study. The purpose of supplementing the required book is to add a perspective that might be more culturally and linguistically relevant to the lives of the students (Harris 1999). Finally, CLR proponents encourage the use of engaging literacy strategies, many of which are connected to oral and written language development.

Responsive Academic Vocabulary

The focus of vocabulary development is building on words that represent concepts that students bring to the classroom. Many of these words come from their cultural backgrounds and from their lives at home and in their communities. Conceptually, these words are connected to academic vocabulary, but the students may not have the academic terms within their vocabulary. To promote students' acquisition of academic vocabulary, CLR teachers focus on effective common vocabulary strategies: wide and abundant reading, contextualization and conceptualization of words, knowledge of word parts, and synonyms. Using the personal thesaurus—a tool first used in the AEMP program—that we have fully developed at CLAS, teachers use activities that build on the students' words. The words selected for the personal thesaurus focus on academic words, those that Beck, McKeown, and Kucan (2002) believe teachers should target for instruction. The personal thesaurus is used to have students expand their academic vocabulary by building on words they *own* conceptually as a result of their experiences at home and in the community. Through a process of synonym development, students connect the conceptual words they have with the academic labels they are exposed to, therefore expanding their vocabulary. For teaching specific content-area words (Beck, McKeown, and Kucan 2002), which in many cases are specific to content areas, we have further developed another tool called the *personal dictionary* based on the Frayer Model (Frayer, Frederick, and Klaumeier 1969). In this activity, students create their personal dictionaries using words learned commonly in mathematics, science, social studies, and other areas.

Responsive Academic Language

The fourth pedagogical area involves the CLR teacher using the process of contrastive analysis or codeswitching in the students' instructional experiences. Contrastive analysis, an age-old second language methodology, entails having students look at linguistic forms in their home language and then translate those forms into their target language. Contrastive analysis can be used with written and oral language. In particular, when using the writing process, this type of analysis can be used during the revision and the editing stage. The idea is that instead of having students "correct" their language, teachers have the students "translate" to the language of school. Students can practice codeswitching or contrastive analysis by participating in sentence-lifting exercises, doing situational role playing, or providing in-the-moment translations from their home language to the target language. For example, a student responds to a question in his or her home language. Let us assume the response was correct. The teacher would then have the student translate the response from the home language into Standard English or Academic Language. Over time, having students engage in switching on a regular basis can be empowering for them because their linguistic behaviors are validated and affirmed while they are learning the benefits of speaking and writing in Standard English and Academic Language. The final subcategory in responsive academic language is situational role playing. Having students practice situational appropriateness through role playing is fun for students. This form of role playing involves students in making language and behavorial considerations based on the audience and the purpose of the communication.

Pause to Ponder

- How does CLR pedagogy strengthen the interrelationship between classroom management and effective learning?

- In what ways do you think instructional activities for academic literacy, vocabulary, and language overlap?

Responsive Learning Environment

Although responsive learning environment does not appear in Figure 2.2, it is an important aspect of CLR pedagogy. A CLR classroom environment is the key in understanding the environmental-behavior relationship that enables teachers to organize and equip the classroom so that situational behaviors are likely to occur (Shade, Kelly, and Oberg 1997). All arranged environments can influence behavior. How spaces are organized through furniture placement, how learning materials are selected, where they are placed, and how the materials are arranged for the learners' use can have profound impact on student achievement. These factors can send strong messages that encourage students to act in particular ways. Surrounding students with a language-rich environment rife with symbols and print that stimulate language development and literacy acquisition enables them to thrive. The arranged environment should provide the spatial context in which movement and learning activities take place. Also, the classroom environment has to provide resources rich in context, in terms of instructional materials. This includes relevant, validating, and affirming high-interest instructional resources that enhance student engagement in the learning process.

The five pedagogical areas are each developed in more detail in the remaining chapters in this book. The chapters explain the overall purpose of each area, describe key CLR strategies, and present a range of instructional activities.

Check for Strategy, Quantity, and Quality of the Pedagogy

The second part of the formula for infusing CLR is checking for strategy, quantity, and quality.

At this stage, if the general pedagogy is present, teachers must then reflect on the extent to which they are already implementing effective pedagogy and to what extent it is working. The standard agreement is this: CLR is meant to add and to enhance what is already working, but if the existing pedagogy is not working, then the agreement is to get rid of it. Consider these examples that illustrate what I am looking for when I check for quantity and quality.

Brain-based research (Jensen 2005; Wolfe 2001) suggests that movement in the classroom is necessary and positive. Providing opportunities for students to move about during class time is a factor for consideration in responsive classroom management. Having students move around the room while involved in instructional conversations provides a different way of learning that is validating and affirming. Movement takes learning from abstract to concrete (Jackson 2009). I prescribe that elementary students should be moving at least two to three times per hour and secondary students one to two times per hour.

Pause to Ponder

- Have you defined how often students should move about during class time?

- How are the movements connected to instructional activities?

Once the teacher has established a guideline of the frequency for students to move within an hour, it is easy to check for quantity in the classroom. The question is straightforward. Depending on their level, how many times, on average, do students move in class? If the teacher has not planned routines and frequencies for movement, I advise that he or she does so in order to be more responsive to the needs of the students. After establishing the quantity, then check for the quality of the movements.

The question now becomes this: If the teacher is having the students move two to three times per hour, what is it that he or she is having them do and, most important, is it working? For example, in a professional development session in which I asked participants to describe movement activities, a teacher described a question-answer relay game. The teacher used the game to review for a test. Individual students came up to the board, and the teacher gave them a question. If the students gave the correct answer, they could then relay the answer to a teammate, and that student would come up to the board. Although the students are moving, the quality of this movement would not be seen as responsive. Simply having one student move to the front of the room to answer questions is not considered instructional movement. The quality of the movement is poor in this example. Better examples of movement activities would be such common activities as Give One, Get One; Think-Pair-Share; or Corners (these and other activities are described in Chapter 3). In effective instructional movement activities, all of the students are moving and are involved in instructional conversations while moving. This type of movement is of higher quality. Overall, if the quality of the pedagogy is working, then we keep it. It is now a matter of adding the CLR layer to the teaching. If the quality of the pedagogy is lacking, then we get rid of the activity and replace it with the CLR layer.

Strategies and Activities to Infuse Culturally and Linguistically Responsive Pedagogy Elements

The final step in the formula is the infusion of CLR activities into the lessons. There are two important questions to focus on regarding the infusion of CLR pedagogy: What makes the lesson culturally and linguistically responsive? What specific activities are to be infused into the general lesson? Thinking back to the examples of movement, the first way to make movement responsive is by including four steps that the students always do when moving.

1. The first thing that students must do when they move and talk to one another is to greet one another in culture-specific ways. We acknowledge firsthand that a greeting is cultural. This greeting comes through a cultural orientation that has been learned at home or in the community, and that has been passed down from one generation to the next. For example, in Black culture, the greeting might be the "soul shake" or what is known as the "Black Man's hug." In a Middle Eastern culture, it might be a kiss on the cheek. Whatever the case, students are asked to culturally greet one another.

2. Move! Everyone has to be in and out of his or her desk. Unless physical limitations or challenges are at play, the

expectation is that all students will be out of their seats.

3. Do the task. The task changes, depending on the activity. For example, in the activity Give One, Get One, the students have a response that they have to give to another classmate (give one); in turn, they receive a piece of information (get one) from a classmate.

4. Students cannot talk to the individuals in their own row or group, or in the group or row to the right or left of them. The purpose of this step is to increase interaction among the students in the class and to ensure that they are not always talking to the same classmates.

These steps represent CLR and movement. Figure 2.3 shows the strategies and activities that contribute to the inclusion of CLR in the areas of responsive classroom management, responsive academic literacy, responsive academic vocabulary, and responsive academic language. These represent the sets of strategies that are prescribed for teachers practicing CLR. For teachers embracing CLR pedagogy, two distinct aspects have to be realized:

- A change in mindset about the students' cultural and linguistic behaviors;

- Intentional incorporation of the strategies into daily teaching.

Fig. 2.3 Infusing CLR into Educational Pedagogies

Responsive Management	Responsive Vocabulary
• movement • attention signals • ways of discussing and responding • collaboration	• selecting academic words and content-area words • focus on key strategies • context • word parts • synonyms • reinforcement activities
Responsive Literacy	**Responsive Language**
• culturally responsive supplemental text • read-alouds as storytelling • effective literacy strategies	• switching • revising • role playing

Prescribing that teachers use the responsive strategies with all students ensures that they will have ample opportunity to learn how to switch between languages or cultures and how to be situationally appropriate. To achieve success, the students must have multiple instructional experiences in which they practice for switching and situational appropriateness. This learning *must* occur through instruction. Lectures, guest speakers, movies, field trips, ethnic food days, ethnic dress days, or anything that superficially addresses multiculturalism or appreciating diversity will *not* produce the desired results. To avoid these surface attempts at achieving situational appropriateness, an action known as *instructional juxtaposition* is necessary.

Traditional strategies or activities can, by default, be defined as teacher centered, having medium-to-high affective filter, and limiting student choice. These activities include what I call *random urgency*. Random urgency is the situation in which any student can be called on at any time and the students do not resist being called upon because they believe the process is fair and random. In contrast, instructional juxtaposition allows students to give verbal responses spontaneously. We refer to this activity as *Give a Shout Out*. Students can "shout out" the responses, but their responses have to be one-word responses done in chorus. For instance, the teacher might ask, "What is the answer for the problem *two times three minus four*?" The teacher would then say "Shout out," and the class, in unison, responds with the answer "two."

Back It Up is another example of juxtapositioning. In this activity, the teacher calls on the students. Back It Up is paired with or then juxtaposed to Shout Out. The latter activity is culturally and linguistically responsive, and the former is more traditional. By experiencing both activities in proximity, the students have practice at switching and situational appropriateness through the teaching and learning. With ample practice over time, students can begin to decide for themselves which activity is most appropriate for them

Instructional juxtaposition is the pairing of a particular responsive strategy or activity with a traditional strategy or activity.

to use, depending on the situation. A series of these types of juxtapositions are empowering not only for the students but for the teacher as well. "When I give activities that are responsive to my students, I seem to get more out of it than they do. It is liberating. It is empowering," a St. Louis teacher commented after using juxtaposition in her teaching. These and other responsive activities are described in Protocols for Increasing Student Engagement in Appendix A.

Summary

Pedagogy plays a critical role in the CLR formula. First, there has to be an agreement on common elements that have to function effectively and efficiently in any classroom. These elements are summed up in four broad areas called *educational pedagogies*. Second, there has to be a measurement of the quantity of the agreed upon pedagogy. Does the pedagogy exist, and to what frequency or depth? After measuring for quantity, we check for quality, or, very simply, is the pedagogy working? If it is not, the teacher agrees to let it go. Now, we are ready to infuse CLR or, as we say in the training, make it "funky." Transforming traditional activities into CLR means involving responsive cultural and linguistic elements, using a variety of activities, and creating many instructional juxtapositions.

Reflection Guide

Think back to your responses to the statements in the Anticipation Guide at the beginning of this chapter. Have your responses changed? Which parts of the chapter did you find most helpful in clarifying your understanding of the pedagogy of cultural and linguistic responsiveness?

_D___ Culturally and linguistically responsive pedagogy is a curriculum. or approach

_D___ In using CLR, I should abandon what I have known to be successful with students.

_A___ CLR strategies and activities can be infused into broad instructional areas.

_D___ All the activities or strategies must *always* be culturally or linguistically responsive.

1. What activities do you currently use that could be described as culturally and linguistically responsive? Do you think these activities are effective? Why? Why not?

2. How could you use the activities *Give a Shout Out* and *Back It Up* with your students? What would you do to help them become familiar with the expected behaviors for each activity?

3. For CLR to be implemented successfully, the strategies and activities are prescribed for the teachers. What is your reaction to the prescriptive requirement for using CLR?

Responsive Classroom Management

Anticipation Guide

What immediately comes to mind when you see the term *responsive classroom management*? Do you agree or disagree with the following statements about the concept?

_A_ Effective lesson planning is the key to responsive classroom management.

_D_ Students' cultural behaviors must *always* be considered in the context of classroom management.

_?_ You consider your current classroom management system to be responsive.

Me Reality
_A   D_ Students should become accustomed to adjusting their behavior to meet the requirements of the classroom.

_A_ The teacher's beliefs about systems of classroom management can affect the nature and quality of interactions with students.

_A_ A permissive classroom atmosphere creates a welcoming environment for underserved students.

_?_ No matter what the circumstances are, teachers should "love" their students.

While the adage that an engaging lesson plan is the best resource for classroom management is true, the need for an effective positive classroom management system always exists.

An effective classroom management system may seem mundane and simple; however, it is actually filled with complexities and intangibles that factor into successful infusion of culturally and linguistically responsive teaching. Before infusing CLR into the management system, teachers first need to assess the quantity and the quality of the current classroom management system. This assessment will lead to in-depth understanding of the strengths and limitations of the current system.

The Three Rs: Rapport, Relationship, Respect

Part one of the assessment is recognizing that CLR does *not* replace ineffective classroom management. Many times, administrators will send teachers to my professional development sessions in hopes that what they learn will change these "poor ineffective" classroom managers into ones that are effective. Isolated CLR training cannot solve the problems of teachers who are unable to manage their classrooms. To some extent, CLR strategies can bolster or enhance the situation in some struggling classroom-management systems that, over time, can lead to improvement. However, what I have realized in working with hundreds of teachers over the past 11 years is that there are undeniable intangibles that have to be present to have an effective system. I have dubbed these intangibles the *Three Rs: Rapport, Relationship, Respect*. These three elements are inclusive of CLR, yet to what extent and depth remain relative to the context. The three elements are described in the following table:

Effective classroom management means that instruction can occur without interruptions and disruptions, that the students feel safe and comfortable enough to take risks—to approximate or make mistakes, and that the environment is conducive to optimal learning (Marzano, Marzano, and Pickering 2003; Marzano 2009).

The Three Rs: Rapport, Relationship, Respect

The Three Rs	Definition
Rapport	Rapport speaks to a special connection between the teacher and the student that leads to an understanding based on concern and care for one another. Rapport is the condition that allows one teacher to be able to banter with students while another teacher with the same students is not able to do so.
Relationship	Building relationships is another intangible but essential component. Teachers who have built relationships with their students are trusted. Trust will liberate the teacher and the student to be what they need to be at given moments. The implication is that there are times when the teacher may not like what a student is doing but has the freedom to manage the behavior because of the trust that exists between them.
Respect	Mutual respect between the students and the teacher has to be in place. The respect for the teacher is very simple. The student has to have the confidence that the teacher can teach. Over time, underserved students lose confidence in the ability of teachers to teach. For these students, the first criterion for respect is based on the teacher's ability to convey knowledge with understanding and sensitivity to the audience. With respect in place, the other two Rs are made possible.

As teachers reflect on the management issues in their classrooms, they need to be fully aware of the nature of their relationships with their students.

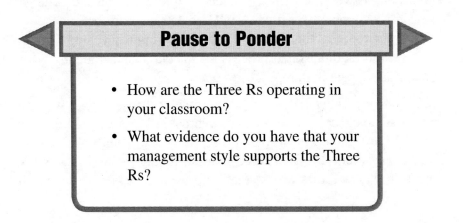

Pause to Ponder

- How are the Three Rs operating in your classroom?

- What evidence do you have that your management style supports the Three Rs?

Classroom Management Schools of Thought

The second step in assessing the current classroom management system requires teachers to examine their beliefs about management practices. The assessment calls on teachers to know the general management school of thought they aspire to as compared to what actually occurs during the course of the school day, week, and year. Emmer, Evertson, and Worsham (2003) describe the three most common schools of thought as 1) authoritarian, 2) permissive, and 3) democratic or collaborative, as it is sometimes called.

- *Authoritarian* speaks to the most traditional philosophy, whereby the primary control of the classroom rests with the teacher. The teacher is literally in charge.

- *Permissive* is on the opposite end of the continuum. Students are not only in control, but they are in control in a way that tends to be negative, confrontational, and creates tension in the environment of a traditional public school setting. In general, students do not like these classrooms, and administratively, they cannot be tolerated. Permissive classrooms are lose-lose situations. However, it should be noted that there are situations where the permissive stance does work, notably some Montessori schools.

- The *democratic* or *collaborative* school of thought best aligns with the CLR approach. Democratic management is a collaborative process whereby a safe, comfortable environment that is conducive to learning is present. The adult facilitates that process for the class, and students participate in that process.

CLR fits best with the democratic approach because it lends itself to student choice, collaboration, and eventual independence. Students need to understand those factors, but they also need to recognize that the teacher is the final voice of authority in the classroom. CLR goes so well with the democratic approach because the approach because the approach garners not only control of the classroom but also provides students with opportunities to develop a love of learning. For CLR teachers, the one caveat is knowing when it is appropriate to be authoritarian. This caveat speaks to the art of teaching, that is, the meshing of intuition and skill. Often, this type of knowing in teaching cannot be taught, trained, or put in a manual. In reality, there are some teachers who intuitively just know when students need to be directed authoritatively and when they need more collaborative guidance. Interestingly, students will respond more positively to the democratic approach infused with CLR when there is an established respect for the teacher, an understood rapport between the student and the teacher, and a developing bonding relationship. When the Three Rs are present, then "going there," or becoming authoritarian is more doable. Teachers who practice culturally and linguistically responsiveness tend to be collaborative in their philosophy, but they also know when to be authoritarian and how to be artful about it.

The Three Ps Approach: Positive, Proactive, Preventive

Part three of the initial assessment is what I call the *Three Ps* approach. Teachers who are intent on incorporating CLR into their classroom management system should subscribe to the *Three Ps* approach: being *positive*, being *proactive*, and being *preventive*. The first P, being *positive*, is the most pertinent to the CLR approach. Showing love to the students for who they are might be the most basic principle for any CLR teacher. By default, to show love, the educator must be positive in vibe and in energy. What does it mean to be positive? It means having a set of uncomplicated and intangible characteristics that are demonstrated consistently to the students—such as care, empathy, sensitivity, kindness, calmness, humor, forgiveness, and patience (Gay 2000). Being positive means not allowing the students' behaviors to turn the educator negative, resulting in such situations where the teacher is not smiling, is not enjoying coming to work, and is not finding the spark that matters so much in teaching. In other words, the teacher has become a negative source in the classroom because of the students' behaviors. A positive stance is best shown in CLR through the use of affirmations—positive sayings, poems, verses, and words of praise.

The second P, *proactive*, is being ahead of the curve in the classroom management game. To stem disruptions in the classroom, CLR educators have to be able to predict potential problems and know where and when trouble can arise. Being proactive entails knowing who the students are and recognizing when occurrences in the yard or happenings in their personal life have preceded (and likely contributed to) what happens in the classroom. Without the teacher being proactive, reactions will rule, keeping the teacher in a backpedaling mode putting out fires. Functioning reactively takes time away from instruction. Proactive behavior beats reactive behavior every time.

The final P is for being *preventive*. In classroom management terms, prevention is the tactic of the teacher choosing his or her battles. The teacher makes the decision either to fight with a student on a situation in an ongoing manner or to deal with it in a way that still sends the message to the student that the behavior is unacceptable but without draining time and energy away from instruction. Typically, prevention can be handled through changes in the classroom environment. For example, the teacher wants the students to enter through one door and exit out the other door. A student refuses to do so and enters and exits out of both doors. The preventive teacher simply locks the one door that students are not to use during the period. When the teacher wants the other way accessed, it is a simple matter of unlocking the particular door. Here is another example that I sometimes joke about in my presentations. If the teacher knows that he or she has a student with "sticky fingers" in the class, rather than constantly observing the student, the teacher can simply clear his or her desk of anything that can be lifted during the time that student is in the class. Do not fight that battle. Using prevention saves time in the long run.

Once the classroom management is assessed and it is known that the three Rs are in place, the philosophy is democratic, and the vibe is a positive, proactive, and preventive one, the steps to a CLR classroom management can be fully enacted.

Pause to Ponder

Think about your classroom-management system. To assess the status of your system, answer True or False to these statements.

1. Your students respect you, meaning that they have confidence that they will learn in your class.

2. You feel comfortable that you can communicate with your students in multiple ways and they "get you."

3. You know your students, who they are personalitywise, where they are from, and what makes them tick and thrive.

4. You have a positive, affirming, caring classroom energy and vibe.

5. Most times, you are proactive with students who could be troublesome.

6. Your classroom environment is arranged in a way to prevent potential classroom management problems.

7. Your classroom management philosophy is collaborative and democratic but authoritarian when necessary.

Answering true to all these statements means your classroom management system is CLR ready.

Separating Cultural Behaviors from Wrong Behaviors

Students coming from a culture—in particular one influenced by ethnicity, spirituality, or socioeconomics that does not match the culture of school can pose a challenge for conducting positive interactions and building positive relationships with teachers. Cultural norms and mores that emanate from the home, the community, and heritage lead to what I term *cultural misunderstandings* and *miscommunications* in classrooms every day. The way people interact with one another, i.e., call and respond, take turns to talk, look at each other, use proximity, and measure time or space conceptually, are all culturally determined and machinated by how these functions are conducted in the home, the family, and the community (Villegas and Lucas 2007). Sometimes, these interactions are not congruent with the expected cultural behaviors of a school. The difference between these cultural determinations and the expected cultural behaviors of a school, largely based in the White Anglo-Saxon or mainstream culture, all too often results in failure for teachers and students alike.

Since these misunderstandings and miscommunications occur for the most part unintentionally, students need to be taught situational appropriateness—the intentional use of the appropriate cultural and linguistic norms for the situation. Through teaching situational appropriateness, no value is placed on any culture, in terms of bad versus good, high versus low, standard versus substandard. The *appropriate* behavior is determined solely by the situation. In order to have success, CLR teachers must be able to deliberate and to decipher between *wrong* behaviors and *culturally inappropriate* behaviors. Teachers, therefore, need to be sensitive to what these cultural behaviors are and why they exist.

Culturally Inappropriate Behavior

Imagine that you are attending a spiritual service of any type. You are a visitor and not a subscriber to the faith. As the service begins, you immediately notice the differences in your usual spiritual service and the service you are attending. Your home service starts with a boisterous praise and worship. People are on their feet, singing and clapping. This service starts with a silent prayer and a calming hymn. Your home service allows for expected interactions with the pulpit through a process known as call-and-response. This service does not. In fact, you have the accurate feeling that if you shout out "Amen," you might be asked to leave. Now, as an observer to this experience, the question becomes *Would it be wrong or simply inappropriate culturally if you were to shout "amen" during the sermon in the context of this service?* The answer to that question is the understanding of how to infuse CLR into any classroom management system.

Sticking with the example, most would say that shouting out "Amen" in a spiritual service is inappropriate given the situation, but not wrong given the spirituality. Clearly, the "Amen" is the right thought and feeling but the situation is inappropriate. My contention is that many students are being punished or dealing with negative consequences because their cultural behaviors are seen as wrong rather than inappropriate. Many times, underserved students are shouting out "Amen" in the classroom, but the teacher sees it as defiant, disruptive, or disrespectful.

In order to change this dynamic, the teachers must believe in the cultural behaviors and be able to recognize them as such. This awareness will provide the opportunity for students to practice situational appropriateness. Instead of being sent out of the room, given a time-out, or being embarrassed in front of their peers, students can switch to the culturally appropriate behavior. This process starts, however, with a validation and affirmation of the base behavior. Notably, the teacher has to know what is cultural and what is not. Fortunately, research provides ample data and support to help educators learn about the commonly accepted cultural behaviors of many underserved students. Figure 3.1 shows the traditional cultural behaviors of underserved students contrasted with the expected cultural behaviors of school, which, for the most part, are directly aligned with the mainstream or White Anglo-Saxon culture (Shade, Kelly, and Oberg 1997).

Fig. 3.1 General Commonly Accepted Cultural Behaviors

Cultural Behavior of Underserved Students	School Culture Behavioral Expectations
Sociocentric	Individualistic
Cooperative	Competitive
Subjective	Objective
Relational	Linear
Dynamic attention span	Static attention span
Sense of immediacy	Standardized
Spontaneous	Prompted

While beneficial in describing a range of cultural behaviors, the research has been detrimental by presenting the behaviors in a dichotomous fashion, keeping the thinking about them divided and binary. My perspective allows for looking at the broad cultural categories in a relative, nuanced, and mundane manner. Rather than looking at the behaviors as one or the other, we can examine them on a continuum that determines their relativity in comparison to general categories that are applicable to all cultures. In other words, the common research presented in Figure 3.1 is too broad, even though it is on target in terms of indentifying some of these behaviors. For an examination similar to the continuum I describe, I turn to the work of Wade Nobles (1987), an expert on African American psychology and Afrocentric perspectives. Nobles posits by implication in his examination of Black culture that all cultures are represented by five general categories: themes, values, customs, laws, and prerequisites. A series of descriptors under each topic comprises the topic and is thus representative of the cultural behavior. Figure 3.2 is an adaptation of Nobles' cultural matrix.

Fig. 3.2 Cultural Relativity Matrix and Continuum

Themes	Values	Customs	Laws (Precepts)	Prerequisites
• Spirituality • Resilience • Humanism • Communalism • Verbal expressiveness • Personal style and uniqueness • Emotional vitality • Musicality/ rhythm	• Respect (elders) • Self mastery thought/behavior • Patience • Race pride • Collective responsibility • Restraint • Devotion • Cognitive flexibility • Persistency • Reciprocity • Productivity • Courageous • Resiliency • Defiant • Integrity	• Belief in God (moral character) • Hard work • Sense of excellence • Sense of appropriateness • Importance of history	• Consubstantiation • Interdependence • Egalitarianism • Collectivism • Transformation • Cooperation • Humanness • Synergy	• Sense of family • Sense of history • Language orientation • Significance of names/naming • Importance of signs and symbols (music and rhythm; dance) • Dietary habits

Each descriptor associated with a general category becomes a point on the continuum to be discussed in terms of the culture's relativity. For example, under the topic of customs, hard work is listed as one of the descriptors. First, looking through the anthropological lens of culture, we can make the safe assumption that all cultures have customs and under customs is the concept of hard work. The scale of relativity, however, says that hard work has more relevance or pertinence in some cultures when compared with other cultures. Some might hypothesize that in White Anglo Saxon culture, hard work is highly relevant. However, if one is to go on the generalized, stereotyped, mainstream media perspective of underserved, when looking at Black culture some would argue that hard work is not seen as very important. Of course, a deep and accurate understanding of Black culture reveals that this perception is not true. In fact, hard work is seen as very important in Black culture. The overall point is that one could take any of the cultural concepts posited by Nobles' matrix and examine them according to the scale of relativity, depending on the culture and the person's knowledge of that culture.

Foremost, the CLR teacher has to recognize that all these concepts apply to every culture in some capacity or another, and that from an anthropological standpoint, no value is placed on them. Consequently, the CLR educator must have a keen awareness of these descriptors as cultural behaviors and how they play out behaviorally in the culture of school. A detailed accounting of each of these concepts is beyond the scope of this book. To learn more about the specific cultural behaviors of underserved students, I encourage you to go to the work of Wade Nobles (1987), Barbara Shade, C. Kelly, and Mary Oberg (1997), and Janice Hale-Benson (1986), to name a few. What is germane to this book, however, is the knowledge of how to be responsive to the cultural behavior once it is recognized as a cultural behavior and not a wrong behavior.

The next step in this process is probably the most important one of all. Once CLR educators have opened up to the possibility of cultural behaviors instead of wrong behaviors, they have to make split-second decisions to determine if everyday common classroom management of student behaviors is cultural. If the behavior is determined to be wrong as opposed to culturally inappropriate, then the response must follow the teacher's classroom management system. The point to internalize is that the decision to be made is the difference in a negative exchange or a positive exchange, an escalation or diffusion, or a student being redirected to on-task behavior or ending up out of class and missing valuable instruction.

Pause to Ponder

Are the following common classroom management occurrences culturally inappropriate or wrong?

1. Student is talking while teacher is talking but in an affirming way.

2. Student is tapping on desk while other students are working quietly.

3. Students are picking on another student.

4. Student says mean and disrespectful things to the teacher.

5. Students are in a collaborative group paying attention to students in another collaborative group.

6. Students are stealing.

7. Student is assertively as opposed to aggressively talking back, trying to make a point with the teacher.

Consistent with the research on cultural and psychological behaviors as well as the responses of thousands of teachers in my trainings, most educators would respond that items 1, 2, 5, and 7 can be culturally related, therefore calling for responses that validate, affirm, build, and bridge. The other items (3, 4, and 6) are considered wrong behaviors and should be dealt with accordingly through the classroom management system in place. When it comes to being responsive to the culturally inappropriate behaviors, the response is for the most part addressed proactively through instruction. There is no prescription for what to offer instructionally. Determining the appropriate instruction is a descriptive process. The section in this book, Resources for Teachers, provides examples of effective instructional practices that are culturally and linguistically responsive.

Validating and Affirming Cultural Behaviors through Instruction

Students need daily opportunities and ample practice with situational appropriateness to become conversant with the cultural behaviors of school and the mainstream society. A way to give students the needed rehearsals is through the systematic use of forms for responding and discussing, strategically incorporating movement activities, effective attention signals for procedural movements, and consistent collaborative group work. Forms for responding and discussing define how some cultural behaviors are conducted within a culture or a community, even in terms of school and the society in general. Cultural behaviors, such as when to start talking when someone else is talking, how long to talk, and what tone to use while talking, can be relative and different for students depending on their home culture. Many of these behaviors are culturally and linguistically determined, for instance, the tone used can differ greatly between the home culture and the school culture. For schools, many protocols are schoolwide (macro-level), while some are classroom specific (micro-level). Some examples of schoolwide protocols include where and how to stand in line on the schoolyard when recess ends, how to move through common areas in the school, and how and where to sit in the cafeteria. Classroom-level protocols relate to the structure of the classroom. Some classroom-specific protocols include when and how to sharpen your pencil, where to place learning materials, who passes out papers, and which learning tools are needed at specific times.

In classroom-management terms, many protocols are considered procedures or routines. Effective teachers are well aware that they need to be clear and explicit with instructions for these routines. There is no expectation that the students know how to do all of these things without first explaining and practicing them. Effective teachers also know that there will be some students who will continue to struggle with the procedures and that reteaching and revisiting the procedures on a consistent basis is necessary.

Ways of Responding and Discussing

Giving students multiple ways of responding and discussing in class is part of the responsive classroom management (Kagan and Kagan 2009). The key is making explicit how to respond in class and how to conduct discussions so that students know what protocol is most appropriate for the response and/or for the discussion. This explicit instruction also enables students to learn why these routines are necessary. These protocols teach situational appropriateness—the types of behavior or participation that are appropriate for a particular situation. In addition, the consistent use of the protocols provides for variation in the types of response and discussion in the classroom, leading to increased engagement overall.

Ways of responding are used to *explicitly* communicate to students how the facilitator or teacher wants them to respond to questioning or instruction as a *whole group*. In other words, the teacher knows the purpose of the question being asked (e.g., checking for understanding, assessing prior knowledge, checking for engagement, volunteering of personal experiences) and clearly communicates how the students should respond to the question. The involuntary ways of responding also encourage accountability and engagement on the part of the learner and provides more accurate feedback to the teacher about students' understanding as a whole group, demonstrated by their need for random participation.

The use of such ways of responding, for example, *Roll 'Em* or *Pick-a-Stick* (see sidebar on next page), establishes a learning environment in which everyone plays a critical role and is validated in the process. These activities are effective in that they convey to students that:

- Their attention and participation are required during whole-group instruction and questioning so that they learn

- They are all integral members of the classroom community

- Everyone's thoughts, ideas, and attention are necessary for an effective learning environment

In addition, the teacher's use of a variety of explicit ways of responding further enables students to be more aware of the need to correlate their participation and behavior with the given needs for a particular setting (i.e., to be situationally appropriate). Various ways of responding should be used throughout the entire day.

Pause to Ponder

Think about how many times a day the whole class is engaged with you or another designated speaker or is responding to your prompts or questions.

- How do you attract and maintain the students' attention?

- What are your expectations for their behavior during whole-class activities?

During all of these times, the teacher already has an expectation of how he or she wants students to participate, whether it is simply listening, silently taking an assessment, answering questions one at a time, or shouting out an answer. Truly, there is never a time when students are not participating in the classroom whether as a whole group (ways of responding) or in small groups (ways of discussing). Protocols for increasing student engagement are provided in the section of this book called Resources for Teachers. Amy Coventry, a CLAS original teacher and current consultant, developed a resource that summarizes successful protocols we have used at our laboratory school and in working with hundreds of schools across the country.

In a CLR classroom, the activities are designed to accommodate cultural behaviors. Figure 3.3 demonstrates matches between cultural behaviors and CLR infusion activities. Several of the infusion activities are those described in Protocols for Increasing Student Engagement of the Resources for Teachers section (Appendix A). By identifying the cultural behavior, the teacher is able to select those activities that are most responsive to student needs.

Examples of Random Participation

Roll 'Em and **Pick-a-Stick** are examples of involuntary forms of responding.

In **Roll 'Em**, students are seated in groups of four to six. The students think about their answers to a question the teacher has posed. The teacher rolls two number cubes. One number cube represents the table or group number and the other cube represents the seat number of a student. The student sitting in the seat represented by the rolled cubes answers the question. The teacher continues rolling the number cube until a sufficient number of answers is given.

In **Pick-a-Stick**, the students think about the answer to a question the teacher has asked. After sufficient wait time, the teacher picks from a group of sticks that represent each student. The chosen student answers the question. The teacher continues with stick selection until a sufficient number of answers is given.

Fig. 3.3 Cultural Behaviors Matched with Effective CLR Infusion Activities

Cultural Behaviors	CLR Infusion Activities
Sociocentric/Interpersonal	morning song (while they socialize and prepare for the day); nonvolunteer (equity and inclusiveness)
High movement	Give One, Get One; Tea Party; Silent Appointment; Musical Shares; Inner-Outer Circle
Cooperative/Interdependent	Numbered Heads Together; Put Your Two Cents In; Three-Step Interview; Jigsaw; Team-Pair-Solo; Partners; Send-a-Problem; Roundtable; Round Robin Brainstorming; Whip Around; Train; Give a Shout Out; Call and Response; nonvolunteer participation protocols (equity and inclusiveness)
Highlighting/Performance	Corners; Roll 'Em; Train (Pass It On); Pick-a-Stick; Circle the Sage; Numbered Heads Together; Whip Around; role plays; poetry slam; speeches
Musical/Auditory	Call and Response; Musical Shares; Give a Shout Out; chants; rhymes
Overlap	Give a Shout Out; Numbered Heads Together; Corners; Tea Party (some greetings)
Purpose-driven	Participation protocols; visual organizers depicting unit activities; Thinking Maps; explicit direct instruction; Morning Report/ Daily Agenda; real-world connections and applications
Inductive	Visual organizers; Thinking Maps; frontloading
Field dependent	Visual organizers; Thinking Maps; frontloading; accessing prior knowledge; personal connections; culturally and linguistically responsive literature/text/content; Personal Thesaurus; Personal Dictionary. thematic instruction

Effective Attention Signals

Effective classroom managers are able to get the attention of their students at a moment's notice. The attention signal is designed to intrigue the students and to motivate them to listen attentively as the teacher gives further directions, transitions to a new activity, or winds down the class. I promote responsive attention signals as a way of creating what Hooks (2003) calls *cultural resonance* with the students. This provides students with something that they can relate to while at the same time brings them to attention. If the teacher has effective attention signals, then adding responsive signals to the repertoire and using them strategically can make a big difference.

Attention signals primarily take place when students are working in collaboration or in discussion. I have found that many teachers will not use collaborative groups or are less likely to have students discussing simply because they will not be able to regain control once the students are "let loose." However, with an effective attention signal system in place, teachers are *more likely* to use collaborative groups and allow students to conduct discussions. I think that this creative opportunity speaks directly to the power of CLR and how it can make a difference in instruction. The caution is that attention signals can be tricky in terms of when to use, timing, or overuse. Attention signals are specific to getting students back during and after an activity but not necessarily for getting students to be quiet. There is a fundamental difference in the two purposes. Lack of understanding of this difference leads to overuse. Wolfe (2001) says that none of these attention signals will prove useful over time because of habituation. Flicking the light switch to get students' attention may work well the first few times, but with extended use, students often will fail to notice or respond to this signal. Kiechelle Russell, one of the original teachers at CLAS and national consultant for CLR training, compiled examples of successful attention signals. Teachers at CLAS as well as teachers who have participated in our training programs have used these signals. Refer to Examples of Effective Attention Signals in the section Resources for Teachers (Appendix B).

Movement Activities

Adding movement activities to instructional activities provides additional sensory input to the brain and probably enhances the learning (Wolfe 2001). Jensen (2005) reports that brain researchers have verified that sensory motor integration is fundamental to school readiness. Indeed, other research has shown that there may be a link between violence and lack of movement (Kotulak 1996). What is the point? Students need to move when learning. Put another way, movement should be an integral part of the learning, which is why it has to be a part of responsive management.

The lesson for educators in this particular pedagogical area is that having students move frequently and with purpose can actually *decrease* management issues in the classroom. This result is due primarily to the factor of increased engagement overall based on the simple but complex principle that when students are engaged, they are less likely to misbehave or be off task. Fortunately, many of the activities and concepts mentioned in this chapter involve movement and can be easily infused into everyday teaching.

Summary

To say effective classroom management is a necessary and required component of the classroom is to say what we already know. CLR is a way to bolster and to enhance any system by first assessing the classroom management system, then, determining the cultural behaviors as such, and finally, using the effective CLR activities strategically. While I offer no prescriptions, an artful teacher can find the balance between being responsive, validating and affirming, and teaching the necessary behaviors to be successful in school and mainstream society at large.

Reflection Guide

Think back to your responses to the statements in the Anticipation Guide at the beginning of the chapter. Have your responses changed? Which parts of the chapter did you find most helpful in clarifying your understanding of responsive classroom management?

_____ Effective lesson planning is the key to responsive classroom management.

_____ Students' cultural behaviors must *always* be considered in the context of classroom management.

_____ You consider your current classroom management system to be responsive.

_____ Students should become accustomed to adjusting their behavior to meet the requirements of the classroom.

_____ The teacher's beliefs about systems of classroom management can affect the nature and quality of interactions with students.

_____ A permissive classroom atmosphere creates a welcoming environment for underserved students.

_____ No matter what the circumstances are, teachers should "love" their students.

1. What are the most difficult situations you encounter with classroom management? How have you attempted to address these situations? What advice would you offer a novice teacher about effective classroom management?

2. What experiences have you had with student behaviors that are cultural based but inappropriate in the culture of the classroom or school? How are these issues resolved in your school?

3. In what ways do the school administration and individual teachers communicate with the school community (e.g., parents, caregivers, interested members of the public) about the distinction between cultural behaviors and wrong behaviors? What information from this chapter can you use for such communications?

4. Protocols for Increasing Student Engagement and Examples of Effective Attention Signals (Appendix A) provide many practical activities that enhance students' engagement in learning activities. Which of these activities do you plan to incorporate into your instruction?

Responsive Academic Literacy Instruction

Chapter 4

Anticipation Guide

What do you think of when you encounter the term *academic literacy*? Do you agree or disagree with the following statements about the concept?

_____ The majority of texts mandated for use in schools lack effective examples of culturally appropriate content.

_____ Typically, anthologies of literary selections include the more traditional and well-established authors of culture-based topics.

_____ Read-aloud activities are most appropriately used with younger students and those who struggle with reading.

_____ Culturally and linguistically responsive activities are substitutes for familiar literacy practices.

_____ People who are unfamiliar with the purposes and nature of CLR instruction may be susceptible to myths surrounding the approach.

Having strong literacy skills—reading, writing, listening, and speaking—is the gatekeeper to success in almost all academic subjects. Have you ever heard of a student being enrolled in remedial reading and taking trigonometry at the same time? Students who are proficient and advanced in reading and writing tend to be in the higher mathematics courses, while students who are struggling in English language or communication arts find themselves in the lower mathematics courses. The discouraging statistics around reading that we have become accustomed to in our schools, tell only half the story. Not only are many underserved students doing poorly in reading but teachers also know that they are doing just as badly in mathematics and other subject areas. With increased literacy skills being key to these students' overall academic success, CLR provides a particular focus on building literacy skills.

CLR addresses development of literacy skills by focusing on two specific areas: academic literacy, which is discussed in this chapter, and academic language, which is discussed in Chapter 6. The focus of academic literacy is done through a lens of text. *Text* refers to all types of print, including fiction and nonfiction and a variety of resources such as newspapers, magazines, journals, reports, and Web media. The following three objectives define the use of text in CLR instruction:

- To engage students with culturally and linguistically responsive texts

- To use engaging read-alouds in the oral tradition of cultural storytelling

- To purposefully use effective literacy strategies responsively

These activities are designed to give students more opportunities to understand the relationships that exist between their experience and the language and concepts they encounter in school. As students become aware of these relationships, they are better able to deal with the demands of the mandated texts. Through these experiences, the students develop academic literacy.

Engaging Students with Culturally and Linguistically Responsive Texts

The chances of finding numerous authentic pieces of culturally responsive text in mandated curricula, commercial basal programs, or the standard content-area textbooks are slim. In general, textbook publishers are doing a better job of representing more cultures in an accessible manner in their books, but these attempts are still largely tokenistic and arrayed with the known authors of the past. Recently, I asked a publisher to send me a selection of culturally responsive literature highlighted in their anthology so that I could prepare for a presentation at a reading conference. Not to my surprise, what they sent were the classic Langston Hughes (1951; 1990) and Gwendolyn Brooks (1966; 1973) selections. Yes, you guessed it—*Montage of a Dream Deferred* and "We Real Cool" respectively. True, these texts are certainly culturally responsive, but they are overused in anthologies. Usually, these texts span several grade levels with the result that over the years, the selections have lost their punch. What underserved students face today is a dearth of culturally relevant selections. The CLR educator cannot expect the state-mandated textbook to be genuinely responsive in nature because it is primarily representative of the institutional hegemony. From evidence presented in the previous chapters, we know that the institution, in this case the textbook, unintentionally recycles the cultural hegemony; consequently, the choice of selections continues to be limited. The only option for CLR educators is to actively plan to supplement the state-mandated anthologies with culturally responsive texts.

The first step in supplementing mainstream text with culturally responsive resources is the selection process. All books with African Americans and Latinos on the cover are not necessarily texts that deal with Black and Chicano culture (Harris 1999). CLR educators must be aware of three types of culturally responsive texts when deciding on which texts would be the most appropriate ones to use with their students. The three types of texts are *culturally specific*, *culturally generic*, and *culturally neutral*.

Culturally specific texts authentically illuminate the experience of the group culturally and not racially. The text realistically taps into the norms, mores, traditions, customs, and beliefs of the culture in focus. There may be a stress on the history of racial discrimination and strife, the struggle for freedom, and an emphasis on racial or cultural pride.

Culturally generic texts feature characters that are members of racial minority groups. However, the selections contain few, if any, details that define characters culturally. The characters, plots, and themes blandly reflect America's "common cultural ground" without exercising any depth to reveal the cultural diversity found in culturally specific texts. In effect, the text could be about anybody, regardless of race or culture, with the exception being the focus on national culture.

Culturally neutral books are the least, if at all, culturally responsive and are *not* recommended as appropriate books. These feature characters and themes that are about people of color but fundamentally are about something else. This type includes informational books that show people from diverse backgrounds engaged in activities from commonly told stories but with different faces. The best examples of these books are traditional fairy and folk tales. For example, *Mary Had a Little Lamb* becomes *Monique Had a Little Lamb,* where the female main character is literally blackfaced, with nothing being different about her other than her color.

To avoid the pitfalls of selecting texts that are culturally neutral, LeMoine (1999) offers the following tips:

- Choose well-known authors, illustrators, publishers, and sellers who have already developed solid reputations for producing culturally appropriate materials.

- Critically analyze how the characters are portrayed in the story, how the facts are presented, and in what context they are presented.

- Evaluate factual information for accuracy.

- When applicable, analyze the author's use of nonstandard language for authenticity and thoroughness.

- Carefully examine the illustrations for appeal, ethnic sensitivity, and authenticity.

The overall goal in the selection process is to find culturally responsive texts of all types that are consistent with the themes, the standards, and/or the content specific topics represented in the mainstream titles. I *prescribe* that there should be at least one reading or interaction with a piece of culturally responsive text to go along with every mainstream title, state standard, or topic covered in the course of a class. It is at times incumbent on the teacher to seek stories, poems, essays, articles, songs, or any text that the students can relate to culturally. The teacher should beware of two challenges they will encounter in meeting this requirement. One challenge is finding the time to search for supplemental texts. At first, it takes a great amount of time to seek out appropriate matches for novels, short stories, and other literature for units of study or themes in the various content areas. If feasible, this type of preparation is better done in the summer months. Finding appropriate resources is the second challenge. However, some help is available. Over the years, CLR educators from around the country have already done some of that necessary grunt work. I along with my colleagues, led by Dr. Letitia Davis, have put together a starter list of culturally responsive texts. In no way is this list exhaustive or meant to be complete. It is simply a nudge to begin the work of collecting titles with the trust that teachers will continue the process based on the particular needs of the students and their context. The list of Culturally Responsive Books can be found in the section titled Resources for Teachers (Appendix C).

Pause to Ponder

- What are the titles of selections you have used to supplement the mandated texts in the subject area(s) you teach?

- What problems have you had to overcome in finding suitable resources to use with your underserved students?

Using Read-Alouds in the Oral Tradition of Cultural Storytelling

The focus of effective literacy strategies is meant to engage students who might be otherwise disengaged, unmotivated, or turned off to the idea of reading as a source of pleasure and entertainment as well as information and knowledge. These three areas enable necessary levels of engagement to lead to increased achievement in literacy and compel students to a stronger desire to read. Reading aloud is the cultural complement to storytelling for many students, including those in the middle and secondary grades. It is a reminder of the elementary years when everyone came to the rug to hear a story from the teacher. While reading aloud has taken some knocks in current research, I still see it as a powerful way to connect to students culturally and build their literacy skills in ways that Harris (1999) describes.

Effective Read-Alouds

According to the National Reading Panel (2000), fluency is the ability to read text with speed, accuracy, and proper expression. Fluent readers recognize words automatically, read aloud effortlessly with expression, and do not have to concentrate on decoding while comprehending what they are reading. Fluency has three components: *accuracy*, *rate*, and *prosody*. In order to implement fluency teaching into reading instruction, teachers need to be aware of the three components.

Reading aloud to students helps them develop and improve literacy skills such as reading, writing, speaking, and listening (Trelease 2001). Research indicates that listening to skilled readers stimulates growth and understanding of vocabulary and language patterns. Reading aloud benefits children for whom standard English is not their first language. Students need daily opportunities and consistent practice with reading to improve their fluency. Reading aloud can help students become more fluent and competent readers. It is important not to put new English learners or nonproficient readers on the spot in read-aloud sessions. English learners and nonproficient readers

Accuracy describes the student's ability to recognize words and read them instantly. As students become fluent readers, they demonstrate automaticity in recognizing words.

Rate is the speed at which a person reads. As students become fluent in reading, they learn to adjust their rate according to the purposes for reading and the nature of the selection.

Prosody refers to stress, intonation, and pauses (known as reading with expression or feeling).

need plenty of time to experience receptive language (listening) while they are becoming more confident with expressive language (speaking and reading aloud). I have included a collection of read-aloud activities in the Resources for Teachers section (Appendix D). The read-alouds can be used to model fluent reading, guide oral reading, and give students opportunities to practice. Each read-aloud is described along with the pros and cons of the activity and an explanation of why it is culturally responsive. The collection includes activities that are familiar to many teachers, for example, *Fade In and Fade Out*, *Echo Reading*, *Buddy Reading*, and *Choral Reading*.

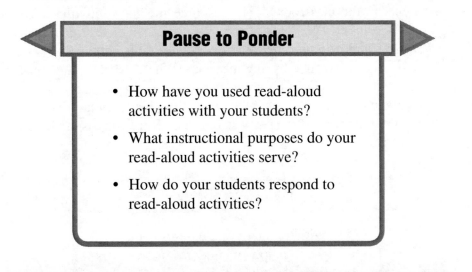

Pause to Ponder

- How have you used read-aloud activities with your students?

- What instructional purposes do your read-aloud activities serve?

- How do your students respond to read-aloud activities?

Using Effective Literacy Strategies Responsively

A common myth about CLR is that the strategies and activities are meant to replace effective practices. I urge teachers to take heed of this caution. The observation is not true in general, and it is not true about effective literacy strategies. Infusing CLR does not mean throwing the baby out with the bath water, as the saying goes. When it comes to literacy practices, teachers must continue to do what they know works for students. The key is to match the CLR infusion with effective literacy practices.

My colleagues and I have culled the literacy research and have identified effective literacy strategies that are well matched with CLR activities. These strategies are particularly well suited to the CLR classroom because they offer a source of motivation and interest to students for the purposes of increased engagement. I have included a collection of Culturally Responsive Literacy Strategy Activities in the Resources for Teachers section (Appendix E). The activities are described, and recommendations for use are provided. I am confident that there are many familiar activities; however, I hope that the descriptions and suggestions for use will provide new insights about how to use these activities with underserved students in the classroom. The resource includes activities such as *Hink-Pinks*, *Thinking Maps*, *Reader's Theater*, *Reciprocal Teaching*, and *Anticipation/Reaction Guide*. This collection is not meant to be exhaustive by any measure. What CLR teachers must do is find the "right" fit for their students and strategize how to effectively implement the strategy with their instruction. Teachers should remember that the purpose of the CLR infusion is increased engagement.

Pause to Ponder

- Which literacy strategies do you use to help your students improve their ability to recognize words, understand concept relationships, make predictions, or summarize what they have read?

- How do you vary your use of these strategies to meet the needs of underserved students in your classes?

Summary

As students advance in school, the materials they encounter in language arts and the content areas present new demands on their literacy skills. CLR activities are designed to enable students to become proficient with the use of text. To enhance their students' learning, the primed CLR teachers must accomplish the following three tasks:

- Consistently and appropriately select culturally responsive texts that supplement the core instructional program

- Effectively use read-alouds, which simulate the cultural norm of storytelling for many students

- Continue to use effective literacy strategies with the strategic infusion of CLR activities

Above all, the teacher cannot lose sight of the fact that strong literacy is the gatekeeper to overall academic success.

Reflection Guide

Think back to your responses to the statements in the Anticipation Guide at the beginning of this chapter. Have your responses changed as a result of what you read in the chapter? If so, what new insights did you gain from the chapter?

_____ The majority of texts mandated for use in schools lack effective examples of culturally appropriate content.

_____ Typically, anthologies of literary selections include the more traditional and well-established authors of culture-based topics.

_____ Read-aloud activities are most appropriately used with younger students and those who struggle with reading.

_____ Culturally and linguistically responsive activities are substitutes for familiar literacy practices.

_____ People who are unfamiliar with the purposes and nature of CLR instruction may be susceptible to myths surrounding the approach.

1. What sources have you used to expand your access to materials that are culturally and linguistically appropriate for students in your classes?

2. How do you plan to use the list of Culturally Responsive Books (Appendix C)?

3. Compare the activities you use for reading aloud with those presented in Culturally Responsive Read-Aloud Activities (Appendix D). Which activities are new to you? How do you plan to incorporate these into your instruction?

4. Which of the Culturally Responsive Literacy Strategy Activities (Appendix E) do you use most often with your students? To what extent do you think the activities are effective with your students? What new activities from this resource do you plan to use?

Responsive Academic Vocabulary Instruction

Chapter 5

Anticipation Guide

What do you think of when you encounter the term *academic vocabulary*? Do you agree or disagree with the following statements about vocabulary development?

_____ Effective vocabulary instruction relies on students memorizing definitions.

_____ The purpose of responsive vocabulary instruction is to enable students to recognize relationships between their personal vocabularies for concepts and the academic terms for those concepts.

_____ Students acquire new vocabulary primarily through indirect approaches, such as reading widely.

_____ Teachers should focus primarily on explicit teaching of vocabulary rather than relying on incidental approaches.

_____ The contexts in which students encounter words affect their interest in words and their motivation to expand their vocabularies.

How did you learn vocabulary in elementary and middle school? Like many of us, your learning of new words probably involved one or all of these steps: studying a list of 20 teacher-selected words connected to an upcoming text in a certain content area, looking up the words in the dictionary, attempting to use those words in a sentence or a story, and taking a quiz on Friday. On the surface, this traditional approach to vocabulary learning makes sense. Students are exposed to words weekly, practice and reinforcement are provided through a variety of formats, and a weekly assessment is conducted for monitoring and support. However, from what is known about vocabulary instruction today, an argument is easily made about the ineffectiveness of the traditional approach (Graves 2006). The time for this approach to teaching vocabulary has long come and gone. I liken the traditional approach to vocabulary instruction to someone bringing an eight-track cassette to a party that is playing MP3 files only and the sinking feeling that comes once the individual realizes there are no eight-track players at the party. The MP3 files of today's vocabulary instruction focus students on acquisition tasks that are robust and authentic. But to say that the approach is proven ineffective and outdated is not meant to detract from what we know is effective and longstanding about vocabulary instruction.

Establishing the Pedagogy

A survey of the literature clearly indicates several principles of vocabulary instruction that should be included in any program or approach (Beck, McKeown, and Kucan 2002; Graves 2006; Stahl 1999). These principles include:

- Providing definitional and contextual information about the word's meaning

- Actively involving students in word learning through talking about, comparing, analyzing, and using the target words

- Providing multiple exposures to meaningful information about each word

- Teaching word analysis

When working with students, especially underserved students, teachers must consider these time- and research-proven concepts. Activating prior knowledge, making schematic connections, and building on the words that the students already know are central to any basic vocabulary instruction. Responsive vocabulary teaching acknowledges that students have a comprehensive conceptual knowledge base rooted in their culture, community, and life experiences that can be used to build academic vocabulary. Plainly put, students come to school with some knowledge. Through their rich out-of-school experiences, students have a multitude of thoughts, opinions, and concepts about the communities they live in and the world around them. More importantly, they have given their own labels, names, and words to these concepts. Students have vast conceptual vocabularies upon which strategic vocabulary instruction can be built.

Responsive vocabulary instruction is based on the following four premises:

1. Students come to school with conceptual meanings of words intact and need to expand their home vocabularies with academic vocabulary.

2. Teachers must focus on recommended key vocabulary strategies for word acquisition, not simple word memorization.

3. Synonymous usage of words needs to be developed, particularly for nonstandard language speakers or second-language learners.

4. Slang, profanity, and racially charged terms can become sources of academic vocabulary expansion, influencing students' word choice and awareness of situational appropriateness.

Students' Personal Vocabularies Are Based on Real-World Concepts

Students bring to school home and community vocabularies that are based in real-world concepts. The intention of expanding academic vocabulary as a pedagogical approach involves bridging the students' world of words to the academic world of words. This bridging takes into account that the concepts are generally the same in both worlds even though the terminology may differ.

Acquiring understanding of the concepts that words represent is different from simply knowing the meaning of the words. Although some teachers have their students use the dictionary to find definitions, this activity is not particularly useful for building students' vocabulary. The dictionary is a reference source to be used judiciously to help students confirm meanings after they have had opportunities to engage in other more productive vocabulary-acquisition activities. Expanding academic vocabulary through an approach that is validating and affirming differs from traditional instruction in that it assumes that the students already have the concepts but lack the academic words or labels. Responsive vocabulary instruction is an approach that validates and affirms the students' vocabulary for concepts.

The building and bridging aspect of the approach is illustrated in the idea of the dimensions of knowing a word (Cronbach 1942). Notably, the overarching goal of vocabulary instruction is for the student to *own* the word, not merely to memorize a definition for it. Figure 5.1 shows the dimensions of knowing a word.

Academic vocabulary includes words that are used in the course of assigning, teaching, and discussing within the context of classes (e.g., *brainstorm, compare, illustrate*), and words that are specific to the content areas (e.g., *poetry, circumference, matter, dictate, narrator, planet, fossil, ancient, experiment, triangle*).

Fig. 5.1 Cronbach's Dimensions of Knowing a Word

Dimension	Description
Generalization	Ability to define a word
Application	Ability to select or recognize a situation appropriately
Breadth	Ability to apply multiple meanings
Precision	Ability to apply a term correctly to all situations and to recognize inappropriate use
Availability	Ability to actually use the word

Pause to Ponder

Which dimension of knowing a word do you usually aim for in your instruction?

After presenting and discussing the dimensions in my workshops, I ask participants which dimension they typically implement most in their classrooms. The almost unanimous response is *generalization*. Keep in mind that this response is in the context of traditional vocabulary teaching in most situations, where there is no uniform vocabulary program in place. In contrast, responsive vocabulary, which validates and affirms first and then builds and bridges, pushes the instruction beyond simple generalization to the other dimensions. The ultimate goal in responsive vocabulary instruction is to lead students to the dimension of availability—the level at which students *own* the words.

Vocabulary Instruction Focuses on Acquisition

A common question that is asked in vocabulary instruction is *What do proficient readers do when they come across a word they do not know?* (Krashen 2004). The point of the question is to show that proficient readers use what I call *acquisition strategies* rather than the dictionary to figure out what the word means (Stahl 1999). Ironically, many times, struggling readers are told to go the dictionary when they come across an unfamiliar word. Such a directive is not an acquisition strategy. According to vocabulary research (Bromley 2007; Graves and Watts-Taffe 2002; Yopp and Yopp 2007), vocabulary acquisition strategies include:

- Wide and abundant reading

- Contextualization and conceptualization of words

- Knowledge of word parts

- Utilization of synonyms

Ample practice with these strategies becomes integral to expanding the academic vocabulary approach.

Krashen (2004) has led the charge that reading often and widely is the best way to acquire vocabulary. This notion is not new, but it is hotly debated in the terms of implicit instruction as opposed to explicit instruction (National Reading Panel 2000). My position is that reading cannot hurt and that both types of instruction are necessary. One does not negate the other.

Graves (2006) provides another way of thinking about how we know words. He defines four vocabularies:

- **Receptive-oral:** words we understand when we hear them

- **Receptive-written:** words we can read

- **Productive-oral:** words we use in our speech

- **Productive-written:** words we use in our writing

Using Synonyms to Expand Vocabulary Knowledge

How we think about word usage can be related to our linguistic background or home language. For some second language learners and nonstandard language speakers, synonymous usage of words is not commonplace. Rather, one word or phrase can have multiple meanings with some nonstandard language speakers. For example, in African American Vernacular English (AAVE), terms like *bad* and *get* remain constant in usage regardless of the ever-changing meanings. In AAVE, *bad* has essentially three uses. There is the *bad* bad, meaning "not good." There is the good or awesome *bad*, as in "That is a *bad* car you have there." Lastly, there is the now commonly said *my bad*, meaning to offer contrition. *Get* has numerous meanings as well; for example, "get down," "get out of here," "get real," "get me a soda," "getting on my nerves," "get it straight," "get your groove on," and so on. Standard English speakers, in contrast, are more likely to change the term with the meaning, therefore employing synonymous usage. For example, "leave here," "be for real," "bring me soda," "you are annoying me," and "dance really well or with intensity" would be the complements to the AAVE example uses of *get*. Responsive vocabulary recognizes this dynamic and makes the instructional modifications, particularly in the instance of second language learners and nonstandard language speakers.

Unique Sources of Academic Vocabulary Expansion

Many mistakenly see slang as completely representative of what a nonstandard language is rather than recognizing that slang is simply part of the vocabulary of any language. In general, vocabulary or semantics is one of the six language dimensions, that comprise any linguistic entity (Levine 2002). The six dimensions are phonics, morphosyntax, syntax, vocabulary, nonverbal languages, and discourse style. Linguists tell us that slang is essentially part of any language. Slang is evident in a myriad of languages including Spanish, French, German, and even Standard English. Slang is not to be confused with certain jargons or technology talk, for example texting or legalese.

A second aspect of slang, for the most part, is the language of young people. (Keep in mind, of course, that *young* is relative.) In broad terms, though, most teenagers and young adults are the primary users of slang terms, not older adults. In this context, I consider slang to be a part of youth culture; therefore, teachers must respond to it in validating and affirming ways so that the students' use of these words can be bridged to academic use in the context of school. In order to do this, though, educators must see the words as positives to be expanded upon, not as negatives to be degraded. If done skillfully, teachers can capitalize on students' use of slang as another opportunity to expand their academic vocabulary.

Assessing the Quantity and Quality of Vocabulary Instruction

What vocabulary program or approach is already in place? This question is central to determining the pedagogy teachers will use to help students develop knowledge of academic vocabulary. Building academic vocabulary as presented here is not a program but a way of thinking about how vocabulary works. Often, when I ask this question in workshops, many teachers surprisingly indicate that they do not have a program in their schools. When they do indicate a program, it is usually provided in the basal program. I cannot emphasize enough the importance of having a vocabulary program in place and augmenting the activities with those I describe in this chapter.

Whether there is a system in place for vocabulary instruction or one has not yet been developed, the next factor to consider is how the words are selected. Is the teacher using the words based on a basal text? In other words, are they preselected by the basal program authors? Or does the teacher have a selection process based on what the students are currently reading? Other variables for choosing vocabulary might include content area and grade-level specificity. The way the words are selected is key because the responsive approach requires the teachers to make a second selection. I have found through my research that teachers are more likely to do this second selection if they are choosing the words. When the words are preselected, there is often a reluctance to choose additional words. This situation, unless addressed, can lead to less implementation of strategies for developing vocabulary.

These two questions represent the assessment of the quantity and the quality of what is currently in place. Once these conditions are identified, it is possible to move to the five steps of responsive vocabulary instruction.

Five Steps to Responsive Academic Vocabulary Instruction

Wilhelm observes that "When we teach a subject, or any topic or text within that subject, we must teach the *academic vocabulary* necessary for dealing with it—not just the words, but also the linguistic processes and patterns for delving deeply into and operating upon that content" (2007, 44). To ensure that students have ample opportunities to acquire academic vocabulary, teachers should follow five steps to plan their instruction. These steps are:

1. Contextualize the word selection or "tiering words" according to frequency and relevance for the topic or selection (Beck, McKeown, and Kucan 2002).

2. Teach the Tier Two, or what we will call academic words, as concepts, not memorized words (Beck, McKeown, and Kucan 2002).

3. Develop synonyms and antonyms using the Personal Thesaurus, a tool my colleagues and I at CLAS have developed based on our work in AEMP.

4. Utilize common vocabulary strategies for meaning development and richer representation as well as for multiple assessments.

5. Develop Tier Three words, or content-specific words (Beck, McKeown, and Kucan 2002) using the Personal Dictionary, a tool my colleagues and I at CLAS have developed.

- What vocabulary-development strategies do you use with your students?

- How do your strategies compare to the ones mentioned in this book?

- What is your favorite professional source for ideas about teaching vocabulary?

Step 1: Leveling Words

The value of Isabel Beck, M.G. McKeown, and L. Kucan's *Bringing Words To Life* (2002) is that the teacher has the creative but informed license to determine what words the students should acquire for a given lesson or text. Given that the teacher knows their students better than the authors of the text do, the selection of words can be customized to the specific needs of the students as maturing language users. Beck defines three tiers for words:

- Tier One words are those that students already know, or common everyday words.

- Tier Two words are those that students should know as mature language users.

- Tier Three words are those that students should be familiar with but will rarely encounter in print or in speech.

For our purposes in CLR, I rename these levels as *everyday*, *academic*, and *content specific*.

The academic words are the ones that should be the focus for vocabulary acquisition in general and also in particular for second-language learners and nonstandard language users. According to Beck, McKeown, and Kucan, academic words have importance, utility, and instructional potential. *Instructional potential* refers to words that can be taught in a variety of ways so that students can build rich representations of them and their connections to other words and concepts. These are words for which students understand the general concept but also provide precision and specificity in describing the concept.

Most basal anthologies provide a list of words that the students should know for each unit, chapter, or story. These words usually are ones that the students will not know technically, and the teacher should cover them through vocabulary instruction so they will be able to navigate the text successfully. What Beck, McKeown, and Kucan (2002) recommend is taking the list provided by the anthology and dividing that list into the three tiers. For academic words, there should be five to seven words that will become the focus of the vocabulary acquisition and instruction. These words are strategically selected based on the fact that they will give the students the most mileage in usage as readers, writers, and speakers of Standard English and academic language in addition to reading the specific texts.

Step 2: Using Vocabulary Acquisition Strategies

In this step, teachers use the three key vocabulary strategies that are recommended consistently by the research (Graves 2006):

- Using context clues

- Memorizing the meanings of word parts

- Developing synonyms and antonyms

Using *context clues* is an important skill that enables students to guess the meanings of words from details surrounding the word in the text. The teacher can prepare sentences or a brief paragraph with the academic words embedded within. Students are called upon to use context clues to guess at the meanings conceptually. Since the teacher is more interested in the conceptual meanings rather than the technical meanings, the students initially are going to provide words that they *own* from their vocabularies. In this activity, at this point, teachers have to keep in mind that the meanings will not be exact matches. If there is doubt about the accuracy of the student's guess, the teacher can help the student determine if the estimated meaning is adequate to move the reader along in the text. If the answer is yes, the student can continue reading. If the answer is no, the teacher should probe more with the students. Figure 5.2 shows a sample context clue exercise.

Fig. 5.2 Context Clue Exercise

Target Word in Context	This is what I think the word means…	What were the clues in the sentence that helped you guess?	My new word for the target word
The assignment was so **tedious** that he started to fall asleep.	boring	started to fall asleep	boring

Using *word parts,* or morphological analysis, is a second vocabulary acquisition strategy important for students to learn. "By separating and analyzing the meaning of a prefix, suffix, or other word root, students can often unlock the meaning of an unknown word" (Rasinski et al. 2007, 21). As a strategy for determining word meaning, teaching students to use knowledge of word parts is effective in that it allows them to use their inductive reasoning skills. Simultaneously, they are building their deductive reasoning ability. Again, teachers must keep in mind that deduction skills are being developed as a result of this process and that exact meanings may not result right away. It is more important that students understand the value of using word parts as a strategy to assist them in determining word meaning.

Step 3: Using the Personal Thesaurus (PT) for Synonym and Antonym Development

The Personal Thesaurus (PT) is a tool to help students develop knowledge of synonyms and antonyms. Here is the description of the process:

- Students read text-selection vocabulary and focus on target concepts.

- Students brainstorm synonyms from their own vocabulary bank, indicating that they understand a concept (it does not have to be the exact meaning).

- Students make a list of synonyms for the target word(s).

- Students place and highlight their alternate word at the top of the chart.

- The target word is added on the line beneath the alternate word.

- Any other academic synonyms are added on the following lines thereafter.

- An antonym goes in the last box(es).

- Students may now utilize their own personal thesaurus during writing.

Figure 5.3 on the next page illustrates an example of the student's Personal Thesaurus chart. The figure shows both synonyms and antonyms that the student developed for the target words *boring, important,* and *hope*.

Fig. 5.3 Sample Personal Thesaurus Chart

Target Words		
boring	important	hope
Synonyms (alternate)		
tedious	key	anticipate
dull	vital	expect
unexciting	influential	desire
Antonyms (alternate)		
interesting	insignificant	despair

Step 4: Using Common Vocabulary Strategies and Multiple Assessments

Teachers are well aware that there are too many words to be taught to students one by one. Furthermore, there is too much to be learned about each word to be covered by having students memorize definitions. Consequently, a variety of methods must be used to develop students' vocabulary knowledge. In this step, students are given multiple opportunities to engage with and interact with new words and to practice the new vocabulary acquisition strategies that they are learning. Reinforcement and practice are essential because students are internalizing new words by making connections and expanding their conceptual understandings. After students have been introduced to the words and worked through direct instruction for vocabulary-acquisition strategies, the teacher provides reinforcement and practice opportunities. Teachers should keep in mind that the goal of reinforcement and practice activities is to make students' word knowledge flexible so that they can both understand the word and apply the word to a variety of contexts. Each activity for reinforcement and review gives the teacher an opportunity to informally assess students and engage in discussions that help students explore the facets of word meaning and consider relationships among words. This interaction will build students' confidence and move them toward assessment readiness.

Assessing what students have learned is the second part of this step for teaching vocabulary. As Beck, McKeown, and Kucan (2002) assert, it is important at the outset to consider the type of learning that is the goal, which will determine the type of assessment given. Vocabulary assessment should always be looked at as an opportunity to develop standardized test-taking skills, which means multiple-choice assessments are appropriate. Multiple-choice assessments give students a chance to practice using context clues and word parts to determine word meaning as well as to explicitly practice test-taking strategies. Multiple-choice assessments, however, do not adequately assess students' deeper levels of word knowledge. There are a variety of activities and assessments that the teacher should utilize to give students the opportunity to demonstrate their knowledge.

For more on common and effective vocabulary strategies, I recommend the work of Janet Allen (1999), Camille Blachowicz and Peter Fisher (2006), and William Feldman and Kate Kinsella (2003).

Step 5: Using the Personal Dictionary to Develop Tier Three, or Content-Area Words

For content-specific areas, such as mathematics, science, and social studies, vocabulary instruction will be different from that provided for academic words. Recall that Tier Three words are those that students will rarely encounter in speech or print. These words are not to be used with the Personal Thesaurus because, typically, students will not have their own concepts for these words. Therefore, it will be more difficult to generate synonyms. For this reason, I recommend using the Personal Dictionary, a tool based on the Frayer model (Frayer, Frederick, and Klaumeier 1969). Figure 5.4 on the next page is a diagram that illustrates the model in a Language Arts class. In the figure, *personification* is the academic term in the content area of language arts. Unlike in the Personal Thesaurus, a technical definition is supplied for the term, and the student has to create an illustration and personal connection. The illustration and connection are the features that provide the schemata as suggested by Frayer. Similar to the Personal Thesaurus, students are allowed to build their own dictionary of content-specific words by turning the Frayer four-square model into a collection of 5" x 7" index cards or *Microsoft PowerPoint*™ slides.

Fig. 5.4 Sample Personal Dictionary Card Based on the Frayer Model

Academic Term	Personal Illustration
personification	
Technical Definition	**Personal Connection**
A representation, usually of an inanimate object made animate	The clock spoke to me directly, saying, "You are late for the show."

The directions for using the Personal Dictionary are as follows:

1. Students can use the Personal Dictionary after building concept knowledge. In the first step, students:

    a. Record the academic term

    b. Describe their personal connection(s) to the term

    c. Add their personal illustration of the term

    d. Associate the illustration either with their personal connection or the technical definition of the term itself

2. Teachers can supply students with personal definition *starters*. For example: *It is a thing that... It was a time when... It is a place where...*

3. Students can add, revise, and edit their definitions as they continue to build their knowledge of the term through other experiences and activities.

Two additional examples of the Personal Dictionary are shown in Figure 5.5 and Figure 5.6 on the following page.

Fig. 5.5 Example of a Mathematical Personal Dictionary

Academic Term	Personal Illustration
adjacent	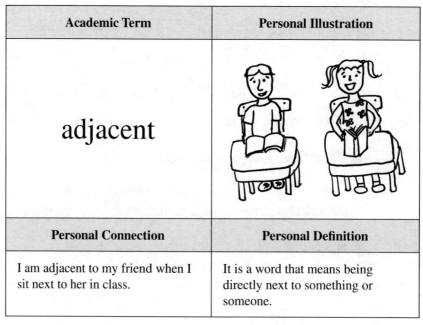
Personal Connection	**Personal Definition**
I am adjacent to my friend when I sit next to her in class.	It is a word that means being directly next to something or someone.

Fig. 5.6 Example of a Science Personal Dictionary

Academic Term	Personal Illustration
atmosphere	
Personal Connection	**Personal Definition**
I see the atmosphere when I look up at the sky.	It is a word that means the part of the sky that starts from the ground and goes far above Earth.

Summary

When it comes to literacy development, the acquisition of academic vocabulary is directly related to larger success in reading, writing, and speaking. Responsive vocabulary offers an opportunity to expand on what the research says about quality vocabulary instruction by adding three enhancements: leveling words, focusing on leveraging strategies, and using a variety of activities and assessments. Similar to what has been presented thus far, the responsive teaching does not supplant the "good teaching" that is being defined. By validating and affirming the concepts the students bring, the intention is to enhance, to enable, and to empower, as seen with expansion of the vocabulary approach.

Reflection Guide

Think back to your responses to the statements in the Anticipation Guide at the beginning of the chapter. Have your responses changed as a result of what you read in the chapter? What new insights did you gain from the chapter?

_____ Effective vocabulary instruction relies on students memorizing definitions.

_____ The purpose of responsive vocabulary instruction is to enable students to recognize relationships between their personal vocabularies for concepts and the academic terms for those concepts.

_____ Students acquire new vocabulary primarily through indirect approaches, such as reading widely.

_____ Teachers should focus primarily on explicit teaching of vocabulary rather than relying on incidental approaches.

_____ The contexts in which students encounter words affect their interest in words and their motivation to expand their vocabularies.

1. What are your preferred strategies for helping underserved students acquire academic vocabulary? What evidence of these strategies is present in your classroom?

2. Fostering a love of words in students is an essential goal of vocabulary instruction. How successful are you in helping your students become "verbivores"? If that word is unfamiliar to you, what strategies are you using to determine its meaning?

3. Which part(s) of this chapter have given you new insights into responsive vocabulary instruction? How do you plan to incorporate these insights into your instructional program?

Responsive Academic Language Instruction

6

Anticipation Guide

What do you think of when you encounter the term *academic language*? Do you agree or disagree with the following statements about language forms students bring to school and the development of academic language?

_____ The needs of students who use nonstandard languages have been ill-served by educational policies that have contributed to institutionalized linguistic racism.

_____ Lack of linguistic knowledge among educators and the public is a major contributor to controversies surrounding the use of nonstandard languages in school.

_____ Teachers have an obligation to accommodate students' nonstandard language in the classroom.

_____ CLR is singular in its recognition of the value of nonstandard languages in enabling students to achieve success in school.

_____ Characterizing nonstandard language as "bad" negates the principles of structure and pattern that apply to all languages.

Of the myriad of topics I cover in my professional-development programs, the validation and affirmation of nonstandard languages, or what I will call *unaccepted languages*, remains the most controversial and provocative. It stands to reason that controversy occurs, because language is arguably the most central and integral aspect of an individual's cultural base and his or her heritage. With that centrality can come hypersensitivity that causes some to become what I define as *offensitive*.

Moreover, discussions about language seem to be coupled with ignorance, misinformation, and entrenched negative beliefs about nonstandard or unaccepted languages. Similar to but different from the other pedagogies that have been described in previous chapters, validating and affirming home language requires the developing CLR educator to have more extensive background knowledge about language. This knowledge is meant to undo the damage of institutional linguistic racism and institutional ignorance about unaccepted languages and language use in general. Notably, *language deficit* is a perspective commonly held about the home languages of students who have been identified as the most likely to be underserved. CLR is designed to overcome the barriers that this perspective presents not only for students but also for teachers, administrators, and policymakers. Specifically, CLR educators must accomplish three objectives in order to be responsive to the home languages of their students. These objectives are:

1. Recognizing the linguistic rules of the nonstandard languages.

2. Giving students ample opportunities for codeswitching.

3. Infusing writing activities into everyday teaching.

Offensitive is a combination of emotions whereby one is being defensive, feeling offended, and too sensitive all at once.

Offensitiveness is an overly emotional reaction to concepts or materials that have been presented unemotionally. In short, a nerve has been touched, and it causes an overreaction in the form of an inappropriate question, a comment or, in rare cases, a behavior.

In achieving these objectives, educators must realize that deficit terminology is unacceptable in the CLR world. Such terms as *fix it*, *correct it*, *make it better*, and *wrong* are frequently used in the context of language deficiency. In CLR, these terms are replaced with such validating and affirming words and phrases such as *translate*, *put another way*, *switch*, *give in school language or academic language*.

In previous chapters, I have defined terms that are central to understanding the concepts of culturally and linguistically responsive teaching. Similarly, I want to clarify the terminology used in this chapter by recognizing that there are many labels for nonstandard languages. To reiterate, I think the disagreement about the terminology used and the ongoing debates about the legitimacy of these linguistic entities contribute to resistance toward and divisiveness about CLR as it applies to implementing the approach to make it part of the school culture. These arguments are futile and become barriers to actual CLR classroom implementation. In order to keep the discussion and progression moving forward, it is best to have clarity, if not agreement, on the terms used. I recommend these terms and definitions be used in CLR discussions. These terms and their definitions are defined in the table on the following page.

Terms Central to Understanding Culturally and Linguistically Responsive Teaching

Term	Definition
Language	A legitimate linguistic entity defined around the parameters of phonics, markers, grammar, vocabulary, nonverbal uses, and discourse styles.
Home Language	The language utilized by family members in the home and others in the community that is different enough from the parameters defined by language from Standard English.
School Language	The language utilized in the context of school; commonly associated with Standard English.
Nonstandard Languages	Not the opposite of *standard language*; only used in the generic context of the term *language*; speaks to the non-acceptance of these language, not to their lack of legitimacy, and linguistically speaking are seen as just as legitimate as the so-called standard languages.
Academic Language	The language used in textbooks, in classrooms, and on tests; different in structure (e.g., heavier on compound, complex, and compound-complex sentences) and vocabulary (e.g., technical terms and common words with specialized meanings) from Standard English.
African American Language, African American Vernacular, or Black English	The systematic, rule-governed language that represents an infusion of the grammatical substratum of West African languages and the vocabulary of English.
Native American Language	The language of Native Americans used at home, on the job, in the classroom, and in other areas of daily experience. It shows extensive influence from the speaker's native language tradition and differs accordingly from nonnative notions of standard grammar and appropriate speech (Leap 1993).
Chicano or Mexican American Language	The systematic, rule-governed language spoken by the Chicano and/or Mexican American community united by common ancestry in the Southwestern United States and/or Mexico.
Hawaiian American Language or Hawaiian Pidgin English	A native speech that evolved as a result of Hawaii's diverse background. It is also called *Da Kine* or, more commonly, *Pidgin* when it really is not a pidgin anymore but actually a creole, or Hawaii Creole English, as termed by the Ethnologue Database. Unlike other English-based pidgin, Hawaiian Pidgin is founded within several different languages, with the Hawaiian language contributing the most words. Still, the term *Pidgin* remains.

Authenticity of Nonstandard Languages

Surprised would be the word that I hear most frequently from educators when discussing the veracity and authenticity of nonstandard languages. Like the general public, educators often exhibit great ignorance about the historical and present-day context of these linguistic entities that linguists have studied for decades.

Corson (1997) revealed that formal educational policies for the treatment of nonstandard languages in schools are conspicuous by their absence in most educational systems. This research aptly points out, however, that these varieties are one way or another brought into the work of the school. Educators have to recognize that students coming from these backgrounds often possess two or more languages that they use in the home. But because of the lack of a formal policy recommendation, often the result is that students are penalized for having a language variety that is different from the linguistic capital that has high status in the school (Corson 1997). William Labov (1972), the grandfather of research on Black English in the United States, argued that there is no real basis for attributing poor performance to the grammatical and phonological characteristics of any nonstandard language. So, why is educational policy lacking in support for nonstandard languages? According to Corson (1997), this absence exists mainly because of simple ignorance about the range of varieties that can and do coexist in a single linguistic space. The point not to be missed here is any language policy that excludes support for nonstandard languages creates a paradox for nonstandard language users and the teachers who teach them.

- What is the policy for nonstandard languages in your school or district?

- What mandates are provided to ensure that the policy is implemented?

- Are sufficient resources available to allow for effective implementation of the policy?

The Nonstandard Languages of the Underserved

Most people view nonstandard languages to be dialects or, even worse, just slang. The research on these languages, which has been a source of vigorous academic debate for decades, strongly refutes that limited perspective. While there is disagreement about the historical derivation of the noted nonstandard languages, there is clarity about the differing views. The views fall into the following four broad linguistic categories:

- Enthnolinguistic perspective

- Creolist perspective

- Dialect perspective

- Deficit perspective

These views represent a continuum of perspectives from most responsive to least responsive, as shown in Figure 6.2 on the following page. This continuum has particular relevance for culturally and linguistically responsive instruction.

Fig. 6.2 Language Perspective Continuum

Most Responsive   Least Responsive

Ethnolinguistic   Creolist   Dialect   Deficit

Each of these categories has a body of research in and of itself with numerous books, articles, and studies readily available. The following encapsulation does not do justice to the complexity and depth of each argument or to the historical context and the relevance to present-day CLR. The *ethnolinguistic* and *dialect* perspectives will be discussed primarily because the ethnolinguistic view is aligned more directly with the concept of validating and affirming home languages; however, the dialect view is that most accepted by educators. The *creolist* perspective offers a worldview, while the *deficit* view is seen as racist today.

Ethnolinguistic Perspective

The ethnolinguistic perspective holds that derivation of the unaccepted languages is rooted in the social, historical, and linguistic development of the people and that any understanding of the language has to be inclusive of these aspects. Essentially, the language was developed through a linguistic process termed *relexification*.

Numerous studies acknowledge that African American students, as well as the other previously mentioned research-identified populations, come to school speaking a language that is dissimilar to but no less valuable than the language of instruction—Standard English. Dillard (1972) estimated that at least 80 percent of all African Americans speak some aspect of African American Language. Smitherman (1998) figured the estimate to be as high as 95 percent. Robert L. Williams (1975), affectionately known as the Father of Ebonics, defines Ebonics as the linguistic and paralinguistic features that on a concentric continuum represent the communicative competence of West African, Caribbean, and

United States slave descendents of African origin. Ebonics does include the various idioms, patois, argots, idiolects, and social dialects of Black people, especially those who have been forced to adapt to colonial circumstances. As a term, *Ebonics* derives its form from ebony (black) and phonics (sound) and refers to the study of language of Black people. This term was coined in 1973 at a conference of Black psycholinguists and sociolinguists. It was not invented during the 1996 Oakland Ebonics controversy. Ebonics refers to the "language family" spoken by Africans throughout the diaspora, which includes Black people in Jamaica (Jamaican Patois) and the Caribbean (Caribbean dialects), South America, Mexico (Black Spanish), and Europe (Black Portugese). In other words, wherever the enslaved Africans were taken throughout the world, some form of Ebonics exists today.

Ernie Smith (1992) views African American language from an Afrocentric perspective. His view is that African Americans as enslaved African descendants are not native language speakers of English. They are descendants of the West and Niger-Congo region of Africa, where a variety of African languages were spoken—Fula, Mandinka, Ewe, and Umbundu, to name a few. According to Smith (1992), research since the 1930s has argued that African American speech is an African Language System—the linguistic continuation of Africa in Black America. Smith says: "African Americans have, in fact, retained a West and Niger-Congo African thought process which is manifested in the substratum phonology, morphosyntax, and semantic lexical structure of their speech. African Americans' native language is Ebonics, a linguistic continuation of Africa in America" (1992, 40). Smith goes on further to say that Ebonics is not "genetically" related to English. Ebonics is not a synonym for Black English. It is in fact an antonym for Black English. The quote from Melville Herskovits (1941, 143) best sums up the ethnolinguistic perspective:

Relexification means that the deep grammatical structure of the indigenous languages was retained over time while the vocabulary of the dominant culture or language meshed, forming a hybrid language of the two forms. For example, using the media-made infamous Ebonics as an illustration, the question is not whether Black English or African American Language is a language.

"This being the case, and since grammar and idiom are the last aspects of a new language to be learned, the Negroes who reached the New World acquired as much of the vocabulary of their masters as they initially needed or was later taught to them, pronounced these words as best as they were able, but organized them into aboriginal speech patterns. Thus arose the various forms of Negro English, Negro French, Negro Spanish, and Negro Portuguese spoken in the New World, their peculiarities being due to the fact that they comprise European words cast into African grammatical mold."

The ethnolinguists' view forges the belief that the nonstandard languages developed without the benefit of the American educational institutions. For the purposes of validating and affirming, as will be shown later, the ethnolinguistic perspective has the greatest potential for impact because it calls for the educator to explicitly acknowledge and affirm the home language as a means to achieving Standard American English proficiency.

Dialectologist Perspective

The *dialect* perspective represents another point on the continuum of language responsiveness. Nieto (1999) defines a dialect as a variety that is spoken because one belongs to a particular region, social class, caste, age, group, or other relevant grouping. Dialects are identified on the basis of the systematic co-occurrence of particular linguistic features among groups of people. For Mexican Americans who are English dominant, for example, this means that their language has rules similar to those of English but manifests some surface variations of the Spanish rules, especially within the phonological component. Varying from the ethnolinguistic view, the dialectologists present what many consider to be a Eurocentric view. Because the rules of the unaccepted language features are always explained in juxtaposition to the English language, the dialect focus is representative of a deficit perspective.

Therefore, terms such as *-lessness*, *weakening*, *omission*, and *reduction* appear in the dialect research. This opposes the ethnolinguistic view, which links linguistic differences to a systematic, rule-governed language with linguistic roots. In the context of school, underserved students who speak a different home language come to the classroom with a dialect that can be *corrected*. Students just need to be taught the appropriate referencing and manner of articulation when it comes to Standard English sounds (reading and speaking) and the correct Standard English syntactical structures when it comes to grammar (writing). In other words, these students can be "corrected" out of their home language. Bilingual education calls this type of instruction *subtractive bilingualism*.

An example of how this view plays out in a structured school situation comes from programs in Hawaii that focus on the home language of Hawaiian Pidgin English (HPE). These programs are bolstered by linguistic research that studies language in a social context in which linguistic differences between HPE and SE are identified. The well-researched Kamehameha Early Education Program has shown marked achievement with this population. These researchers concluded that the culturally congruent style of discourse management was more effective, as it led to more productive achievement-related behavior by the students on a variety of measures. Similarly, the researchers determined that culturally congruent participation structures in the classroom not only foster reading achievement but also facilitate the development of spoken Standard English as well (Nieto 1999).

Subtractive bilingualism is commonly known as when learning a second language interferes with the learning of a first language. The second language replaces the first language.

The dialectologist view is the mostly widely held perspective by linguists, educators, and the general public. For example, in terms of the current stage of research concerning the linguistic variety most commonly known as Chicano English, the dialectologist view categorizes this linguistic variety as a contact "dialect" because it emerges in the linguistic setting where there is contact between

Mexican Spanish and American English. Carmen Fought (2003), a prominent researcher of Chicano English, maintains that while Chicano English is a contact dialect, it is not truly a creole, since creoles generally emerge from a setting where multiple languages are involved.

Creolist and Deficit Perspectives

The other two views—creolist and deficit—are worth noting rather than offering full explanations. The creolist position is very similar to that of the ethnolinguists, with the difference being that creolists do not necessarily attribute the grammatical base to the indigenous language. They see it more as a pidgin that over two generations creolized into solidified linguistic entity. The deficit perspective simply holds that nonstandard languages are nothing but bad or improper English and the speakers of the nonstandard languages are incapable cognitively of mastering Standard English. On the surface, this view is easily refuted and today is seen as blatantly racist. At a deeper level, the reality is that up until the 1940s, this perspective was commonly held and had become institutionalized knowledge. Ambrose Gonzales (1922), a noted deficit linguist, theorized that this should have happened is not surprising, for it is a linguistic axiom that when two groups of people who have different languages come into contact—the one on a relatively high, the other on a relatively low cultural level—the latter adapts itself freely to the speech of former, whereas the group on the higher cultural plane borrows little or nothing from that on the lower.

Linguistic Absolutes

Regardless of the differing perspectives in the linguistic research, the following three agreed-upon linguistic absolutes are evident:

1. All language is good. Conceptually and linguistically speaking, there is no such thing as a *bad* language. Languages are not inherently bad, improper, wrong, or

incorrect. In CLR, these terms are considered deficit in nature and useless with an affirmative position on language.

2. All linguistic forms are rule governed and patterned. They are not haphazard, made up, randomized, or created by rappers. The range of these rules covers all dimensions of language—phonics, morphemes, syntax, semantics, pragmatics, and discourse. Indeed, the fact that there are rules in each of these dimensions speaks to the veracity of the linguistic entity.

3. We acquire the language that is spoken by the primary caregivers at home, beginning at prebirth and continuing up to prekindergarten. In fact, the language that is spoken at home will be the language the student uses at school. The student comes to school with all the rules of that language intact and, most importantly, with a positive view of the language. Unfortunately, the beginning of school chips away at that positive view as all of sudden students are told that the way their grandparents, uncles, siblings, and parents speak is wrong.

To be CLR, the educator has to subscribe to these absolutes, as they are the first steps to being able to validate and to affirm the students' home languages.

Nonstandard Language Rules

With the shift in mindset about unaccepted languages and acceptance of the three absolutes in place, the process of validation and affirmation can begin for the CLR educator. Similar to the examination of culture presented in Chapter 1, what exactly the teacher must validate and affirm needs to be made clear in the context of nonstandard languages. Therefore, CLR educators need to become aware of the researched-based linguistic rules or features of the nonstandard languages so as to know what is worth validating and affirming. The rules are based on a formula of understanding that has three parts.

- Part one of the formula is to lose the hegemonic view of Standard English, meaning that just because Standard English has certain usage or structure as a rule does not mean that all languages have it as a rule.

- Part two is to understand the derivation of the rule in the context of the indigenous language. In other words, it must be recognized how the rule came into existence, especially in comparison to the Standard English rules.

- The last part of the formula is to appropriately codeswitch— or to translate from the home language to the target language—or in some cases make reverse translations.

These aspects of understanding linguistic absolutes are clarified in two examples based on features of African American Vernacular English (AAVE): the habitual BE form and multiple negation.

Fig.6.3 Habitual BE form

Example 1

Name and Explanation of Rule in AAVE: Habitual BE (commonly made fun of or ridiculed by mainstream media when discussing Ebonics). The BE form is typically formed with

- Be + verb ending in –ing

- Be + adjective

Examples: *I be late to work* or *She be playing Bingo a lot at the casino*.

Standard English Rule: The use of *be* in this form does not exist.

Standard English Equivalent: Appropriate tense of the verb "to be" in Standard English in addition to an adverb that describes time frequency (e.g., always, usually, normally, often, frequently).

Translation: I *am always* late to work. She *frequently plays* Bingo at the casino.

Fig.6.4 Multiple Negation

Example 2

Name and Explanation of Rule in AAVE: Multiple Negation

- Multiple negation refers to the use of multiple negative words in a sentence.

- With multiple negation, the more negative words in a sentence, the greater the negative sentiment being expressed by the speaker.

- The negative words act as intensifiers, words like *any*, *none*, *no*, *either*, and *some*.

- An intensifier heightens or lowers the intensity of meaning of an item.

Examples: *I do not have no pencil for you* and *She won't never share her snacks.*

Standard English Rule: Multiple negatives are not allowed. In Standard English, the rule is called *double negative*. Standard English grammar rules dictate that a sentence can only have one negative word. Two negative words, double negatives, cancel each other out; therefore, expressing a positive sentiment. Intensifiers are considered adverbs and adjectives.

Translation: I *do not* have any pencils for you. She *never* ever shares any of her snacks.

Teachers should familiarize themselves with language rules that apply to the languages that their students use. For reference and awareness, language rules as they apply to African American Language (AAVE) and Mexican American Language (Chicano English) are presented in Figure 6.5 and Figure 6.6, respectively.

Fig. 6.5 African American Language (AAVE) Common Rules List

Categories	Examples
Sounds	**Sounds**
/th/ Sound (digraphs)	<u>Dis</u> is my <u>mouf</u>.
Consonant Clusters	I put my <u>tes'</u> on your <u>des'</u>.
Vowels Short /ĕ/ and Short /ĭ/	I am <u>tin</u> years old.
Reflexive /r/ Sound or /er/ Sound	<u>Yo</u> <u>sista</u> is Ca'ol. Did you <u>caw</u> me?
Markers (Morphemes)	**Markers (Morphemes)**
Past Tense Marker "ed"	He <u>visit</u> us yesterday.
Possessive Marker	That is my <u>sister</u> bike.
Plural Marker	I have 25 <u>cent</u>.
Syntax	**Syntax**
Multiple Negation	He <u>don't</u> have <u>none</u>.
Habitual *Be*	She <u>be</u> mean.
Topicalization	That <u>boy he</u> funny.
Present Tense Copula Verb	She pretty.
Regularized Patterns	**Regularized Patterns**
Reflexive Pronoun	He hurt <u>hisself</u>.
Present Tense Singular Verb	He <u>run</u> fast.
Past Tense Singular Verb	We <u>was</u> here.

Fig. 6.6 Mexican-American (Chicano English) Common Rules List

Categories	Examples
Sounds	**Sounds**
/th/ Sound (digraphs)	<u>Dis</u> teecher is mean.
Final Consonant Clusters and Medial Consonant Clusters	I <u>lef</u> my game over there. My dad went to da <u>harware</u> store.
Vowels Short /ĕ/ and Short /ĭ/	I don't got a <u>pin</u>.
/z/ and /v/ Sounds	The firemen <u>safed</u> many <u>lifes</u>. He won da <u>price</u> at the fair.
Circumflex Intonation (Nahuatl influenced)	<u>Doon't</u> bee <u>baaad</u>!
Breath H (Nahuatl influenced)	My hair was all <u>hwite</u>, so I dyed it.
Stress Patterns	I get paid <u>tooday</u>.
Markers (Morphemes) Phonologically Influenced	**Markers (Morphemes) Phonologically Influenced**
Past Tense Marker *ed*	She <u>move</u> to San Diego.
Morphological Sensitive Rule (*thuh* before consonant/*thee* before a vowel)	We saw <u>thuh</u> ocean over there.
Plural Marker (dropped when forming a separate syllable)	He always <u>ditch</u> school.
Syntax	**Syntax**
Multiple Negation	She <u>don't</u> like <u>nobody</u>.
Intensifiers	Mom was <u>all</u> lost on the way to my Tia's. This DVD <u>barely</u> came out.
Topicalization	My <u>brother he's</u> going to the movies.
Present Tense Copula Verb	This<u>…</u>a school.
Prepositional Variation	He was sitting <u>in</u> the couch.
Regularized Patterns	**Regularized Patterns**
Indefinite Article	Do you want <u>a</u> ice cream?
Present Tense Singular Verb	He <u>jump</u> rope to get in shape.
Pronoun	Now they can do it by <u>theirselves</u>.

Effective Instructional Practices

Familiarity with common rules in nonstandard languages enables CLR educators to know what to validate and affirm in their students' languages. Furthermore, such knowledge ensures that the teachers do *not* react negatively to the students' use of home language. The positive steps teachers take to help students build and bridge to the language of school negate the deficit view of nonstandard language. Such terms as *fix it, correct it, speak correctly*, or *say it like you make sense*, which are examples of deficit terminology, should not be used in CLR. These terms must be replaced with affirmative expressions such as *translate, put another way, switch, say in school language or academic language*. CLR instruction enables students to learn how to switch from their home language to the language of school, or academic language. However, that instruction has to in the first place consider whether the student has the skill set to switch. Many students lack the necessary skills, and this lack becomes failure on the part of the school. Although many students, particularly older ones, quickly conceptualize what is needed to switch to the appropriate language for the situation, this awareness does not mean that they will actually be able to switch.

Pause to Ponder

- In what ways do you validate and affirm your students' languages?

- How do you build their skill and confidence in switching to school language?

Contrastive Analysis

Language codeswitching, known academically as *contrastive analysis*, is the practice of comparing and contrasting the linguistic structure of two languages. This strategy facilitates acquisition of Standard English by increasing students' awareness of the differences (rules) between the languages they bring from home and the language of school. Research shows three benefits of contrastive analysis to students:

1. It increases students' ability to recognize the differences between Standard English and the language of Standard English Learners (SEL).

2. Students become more proficient editing grammar, vocabulary, and syntax in their work.

3. Students gain greater facility in the use of Standard English in both oral and written expression.

Many of the instructional activities in Figure 6.7 on the following page are based in contrastive analysis and vary as necessary for the content and/or the grade level. Reading/language arts and social studies provide more opportunities for sentence lifting and retellings, while other content areas, including mathematics and science, are more geared toward role playing and teachable moments.

Fig. 6.7 Language Switching Activities

Activity	Definition
Sentence Lifting	*Sentence lifting* is the use of literature, poetry, songs, plays, student-elicited sentences, or prepared story scripts that incorporate specific contrasts of home- and target-language rule forms. The student performs the contrastive analysis translations to determine the underlying rules that distinguish the two language forms. For example, teachers commonly take lines of rap music and the students change those lines into standard English and then have students analyze the sound difference, effect on audience, or focus on grammar structure.
Retellings	Students first listen to a selection presented in the target language. Then, they use their home language to retell the story or piece of text. The student's retelling is taped so that it can be compared and contrasted with the language of the text.
Role Playing	Role playing gives students opportunities to practice situations through acting and writing with the targeted language. The emphasis is on situational appropriateness, which calls on students to weigh the language most suited to the environment, audience, purpose, and function.
Teachable Moments	Teachable moments are a form of contrastive analysis in which the teacher elicits spontaneous verbal responses from the students about material read or presented, creating on-the-spot opportunities for situational appropriateness in the classroom.

Dr. Jamila Gillenwaters uses role-playing contrastive-analysis exercises with students in the upper-elementary grades. The scenario below is an example of such an exercise that provides an opportunity for students to practice, making choices for which statement is most appropriate given the situation. The activity is based on the AAVE *Habitual BE* rule described in Figure 6.3.

Fig. 6.8 Example of Habitual BE Rule

Boss: Joshua, we're looking for a prompt employee. Do you usually get to work on time?

Joshua: Yes, sir! I don't never be getting to work late.

Boss: What kind of work habits do you have?

Joshua: I be trying my hardest to do good work.

Boss: Do you usually complete your work assignments on time?

Joshua: My employers be impressed with my work.

Boss: How do you normally get along with your coworkers?

Joshua: My coworkers be liking me a lot.

Boss: If we hire you, when will you have time to study?

Joshua: I be studying on the weekends.

Another example of a contrastive analysis exercise is presented on the following page. Based on the AAVE *multiple negation* rule described in Figure 6.4, this activity requires students to categorize the expressions according to home language or school language.

Fig. 6.9 Example of Multiple Negation Rule

School Language or Home Language?

Directions: Read each of the following sentences with a partner. Decide if the sentence is written in School Language or Home Language.

- José never ever messes with anybody.

- We don't never go nowhere on the weekend.

- I didn't go anywhere this weekend.

- Girls won't never play fair!

- You don't ever have any money!

- Why won't boys ever play fair?

- You don't never have no money!

- Nobody better not mess with José!

These kinds of exercises are usually presented in the form of worksheets, which are often criticized as another type of "drill and kill" activity. Although this may be a fair criticism, the value of such exercises cannot be overlooked. As students work to complete the activities, they are gaining experience in analyzing language forms as well as interacting with one another. Obviously, it is the nature and purpose of the activity that is important, not the format.

Sentence lifting, retelling, role-playing, and teachable-moment activities are effective in helping students recognize the similarities and differences between their home language and that of school. I recommend that teachers routinely use such activities, varying them according to subject area or grade level. Importantly, the choice of activity should be based on the instructional needs of the students. When CLR teachers observe opportunities for students to build on their home language to learn Standard English, they should provide lessons that capitalize on the situation. Beginning with validation and affirmation of the students' home languages, teachers can best meet the learning needs of underserved students.

Using Effective Writing Strategies

Writing activities are another way to provide students with opportunities to develop skill in language switching. Once CLR teachers are familiar with the linguistic features of their students' home languages, they are equipped to develop lessons that accommodate these features in the context of standards-based instruction. The writing activities that I describe are examples of those that my colleagues and I have culled from research and have used successfully at our laboratory school. These activities are described in the section Suggested Writing Activities (Appendix F) of this book.

Summary

Responsive academic language instruction is designed to enable students to learn how to move from their home language to the language of school. To develop appropriate instructional activities, CLR teachers have to be informed about the nature of nonstandard language and subscribe to a belief system that validates and affirms the use of such language. In doing so, teachers will play a pivotal role in eliminating institutional rejection of nonstandard languages that has resulted from the hegemony of Standard English in schools.

Reflection Guide

Think back to your responses to the statements in the Anticipation Guide at the beginning of the chapter. Have your responses changed as a result of what you read in the chapter? What new insights did you gain from the chapter?

_____ The needs of students who use nonstandard languages have been ill-served by educational policies that have contributed to institutionalized linguistic racism.

_____ Lack of linguistic knowledge among educators and the public is a major contributor to controversies surrounding the use of nonstandard languages in school.

_____ Teachers have an obligation to accommodate students' nonstandard languages in the classroom.

_____ CLR is singular in its recognition of the value of nonstandard languages in enabling students to achieve success in school.

_____ Characterizing nonstandard language as "bad" negates the principles of structure and pattern that apply to all languages.

1. What have you observed about your students' use of nonstandard language forms? How have you incorporated information from your observations into your lesson planning?

2. Which section of this chapter has had the most dramatic effect on your thinking about responsive academic language instruction? How will you use the insights you have gained to strengthen your teaching?

Creating a Responsive Learning Environment

Chapter 7

Anticipation Guide

What do you think of when you encounter the expression *responsive learning environment*? Do you agree or disagree with the following statements about the classroom learning environment?

_____ The traditional classroom structure with students sitting in rows is most effective in maintaining discipline with underserved students.

_____ Excessive use of decorative materials in the classroom can be distracting for underserved students.

_____ An inviting classroom environment encourages students to interact positively with one another and the teacher.

_____ Learning centers are necessary in primary-grade classrooms but are not essential for students in the upper grades, notably middle and secondary levels.

_____ Fair and clear procedures for classroom behaviors contribute to a sense of community in the classroom.

_____ A combination of teacher-directed and student-centered activities is needed to maintain a responsive learning environment.

Creating a positive learning environment is actually the first step teachers should take as they strive to create a classroom that is culturally and linguistically responsive. Given the importance of this factor, teachers may be wondering why I have left this topic to the last chapter of the book. My reasoning is that the concepts underlying a responsive learning environment are implicit in every aspect of CLR pedagogy described in previous chapters. The absence of a positive climate in the classroom makes it impractical, or more likely impossible, for teachers to implement the strategies that foster and enhance learning for underserved students. A responsive learning environment is one that conveys respect for every student, notably respect for the knowledge, experiences, and language students bring to the classroom. Such a context is central to validating and affirming students' home language as well as building and bridging their efforts to use school language.

Understanding the relationship between the environment and behavior enables teachers to organize and to equip the classroom so that optimal learning is more likely to occur. According to Barbara Shade, C. Kelly, and M. Oberg (1997), an inviting learning environment establishes a pleasant physical and psychological atmosphere that welcomes students. How the students will function within the particular environment depends on their comfort level. Moos (1979) said that for students of color and families of immigrants, their initial assessment of their acceptance into the school environment depends on whether or not they perceive pictures, symbols, and other visual representations that remind them of their homes, communities, and values.

Features of an Effective Learning Environment

Danielson (2007) describes a framework for teaching in which she identifies five broad areas for an effective learning environment. The five areas include purpose, student engagement, curriculum and pedagogy, assessment for student learning, and classroom environment and culture.

Organization of physical space can influence behavior and learning. Conspicuous features including furniture placement, learning materials, bulletin boards, use of technology, and spatial viewing capacity can have a profound impact on the students by sending strong messages for powerful learning.

All learners, but especially underserved learners, thrive in environments that stimulate language development and literacy acquisition and surround them with a language-rich environment rife with symbols and print. The strategically arranged environment creates the spatial context in which movement and learning activities can take place. Also, the optimal environment provides resources that are rich in context and instructional materials, which include relevant high-interest instructional resources to enhance student engagement in the learning process.

Pause to Ponder

- What impression do you think visitors have of the learning environment in your school or classroom?

- What words would you use to describe the climate in the school?

Evidence of a Responsive Learning Environment

My experience with working in numerous classrooms across the country as well as evidence from research (Murphy 2009) provides the context for describing features of a responsive learning environment. *Responsive* here means that which validates and affirms the students in the environment—*not* what remediates them. Through the work of my colleagues at our laboratory school and my professional-development work with thousands of teachers, we have developed a formula for what a responsive learning environment should be. In general, we strive to provide a welcoming environment that has evidence of the students' perspectives and lives.

The many visitors who have come to CLAS have noted and been awed by the exemplary learning environment. Dr. Rebecca Powell (in press), professor at Georgetown University in Kentucky, acknowledged:

> "Throughout the building and in all of the classrooms, there was affirmation of the African American community. Pictures on walls reflected their culture and community. In one hallway, we saw a chart that compared Ebonics structures with Standard English structures, clearly the result of a lesson (or perhaps even a series of lessons) that validated their language while comparing it to the language of power. In a first grade classroom we visited, the class had developed brainstorm webs of "My Community Place" that examined students' special places in the community. The classrooms had what we would call a "print rich" environment, with hundreds of books of various genres, all of which had Black protagonists."

Dr. Powell's observations are a tribute to the ongoing efforts of CLAS faculty in creating and sustaining a responsive learning environment.

As witnessed by Dr. Powell and other visitors, the CLR recipe for a responsive learning environment is framed around eight elements:

1. **Print-Rich Environment:** 70 percent authentic and 30 percent commercially produced

2. **Learning Centers:** reading, writing, listening, math, science, and cultural

3. **Culturally Colorful:** ethnic cloths, prints, artwork, and artifacts

4. **Arranged Optimally:** allowing for presentations, movement, and teacher and student space

5. **Multiple Libraries:** cultural, multicultural, content specific, reading level, and signature literature

6. **Use of Technology:** utilized and prominently displayed

7. **Relevant Bulletin Boards:** cultural, student work, current unit, current events, and content-area oriented

8. **Displayed Student Work and Images of Students:** current, ample, and unit-related

These ingredients are to serve as they would for an actual recipe—meaning that in order to create the dish, the cook absolutely needs these ingredients. However, the exact amount and mixture of the ingredients are left up to the cook's creativity, intuition, and experience. This intentional flexibility is allowed in order to support the customization of the learning environment to the students for each situation. In other words, the responsive environment should not be cookie-cutter or branded. Even though the components are prescriptive and defined, how the environment will ultimately look is descriptive, dependent, and highly reliant on the CLR teacher to think out of the box. The teachers at our laboratory school in Los Angeles use these components in their own way with the result that each classroom looks completely different. In the next sections, I describe the features of a responsive learning environment along with photos of CLAS classrooms. These photos will help you appreciate how a responsive environment is put together.

Print-Rich Environment

The importance of a print-rich environment has been well documented. Students need the exposure to letters and words that is provided in a word-rich environment. For content-specific classrooms, the environment should be deluged with print representations of the content areas. Students should walk into the room and immediately know the content area or know the various subjects in an elementary classroom. Traditional markers such as signs, symbols, characters, and word walls make significant differences for both early readers and struggling readers.

Learning Centers

Learning centers are commonly recommended for creating an effective room environment. Thinking beyond the traditional centers such as reading, writing, or science is key for this ingredient. Centers that feature culturally related speaking and listening activities are welcome additions to traditional centers. A litany of research has demonstrated how audio—namely music—helps to stimulate the brain. Cultural music, ranging from the Native American flute to American Jazz can set the tone and assist in learning. Cultural centers featuring items students have brought from their home and community are strongly encouraged. In these centers, students have opportunities to write about the artifacts and, of course, *show and tell* on a frequent basis. The center acts as a living museum for the class and becomes a source of unity as all students, regardless of their culture, are expected to contribute. Here, it is important to think broadly beyond ethnicity in developing resources for the center. That breadth of the culture center should include youth, socioeconomic, gender, and religious representations.

Culturally Colorful

What colors come to mind when you think of a school? Are you thinking drab, dark, gray, plain, solid? Culturally responsive classrooms are just the opposite of what the traditional colors of a school may be. Bright, dynamic, lively, and inviting colors are characteristic in CLR classrooms. These colors exude fun, student friendliness, and excitement about learning. An inviting classroom focuses on the use of color, lighting, and sound. Here, it is well thought to steal a page from the business world, where the manner in which the environment can actually facilitate employee productivity has been well documented.

This can be the case for classrooms as well. For example, according to Shade, Kelly, and Oberg (1999), Native American cultures seem to prefer earth-tone colors and in some cases bright yellows and pastels. All these colors denote activity and vibrancy. Some CLR teachers have been known to request new colors in their classrooms or even offer to paint their own rooms during the summer months, with permission. The point, in this case, is that color does make a difference.

Fig. 7.1 Example of a Culturally Colorful Classroom

Arranged Optimally

How to arrange the desks, tables, and/or chairs is one of the toughest decisions for teachers to make. Many teachers probably go through several iterations of room configurations during the course of the year before actually deciding on one or two that are optimal. In truth, there is no one configuration that can be prescribed. Whatever the arrangement, it should promote movement, viewing capability, and space (as in breathing room) for the students and teacher alike. The arrangement of desks and tables speaks to the importance of interpersonal relationships in the class among the students as well as between the students and the teacher.

Research suggests that, in addition to the spatial accommodation for collaborative groups, it is just as important to have space whereby the students can connect individually with the teacher. Both of these components allow for a feeling of community, connectivity, and collaboration. Student proximity can affect the reception of verbal and nonverbal cues, which then influence positive or negative classroom behaviors (Good and Brophy 1977). For instance, Mexican American students often view each other as natural resources to accomplish their tasks and offer assistance to peers. Depending on the room arrangement, it may or may not be possible for these students to engage in such actions.

Multiple Libraries

In addition to a print-rich environment, CLR classrooms should first and foremost have large quantities of books organized in multiple libraries. The multiple libraries can be formulated through a variety of categories, such as genres, authors, topics, or reading levels. How the books are displayed is important as well. Similar to the notion of the culturally colorful classrooms, libraries that are set up in a way that is inviting and enticing to students can make all the difference. The appeal of the display can bring a student to the library, whereas the opposite effect may actually keep students away from the library. The more books the better, and the more variety of books, the better, especially for underserved students who are not readers per se. Again, with variety in mind, I am insisting that teachers think beyond race and ethnic identity. Think about books in terms of gender, social status, youth-appropriate, and economic levels.

Fig. 7.2 Example of a Classroom Library

Use of Technology

The pervasive use of technology is hard to miss in the typical classroom today. Many classrooms now come equipped with LCD projectors, document readers, and interactive whiteboards, not to mention laptops for the students and the teachers. How the technology is set up and utilized with the instruction can be responsive, especially if the technology is infused into the instruction with transparency and frequent utilization.

Fig. 7.3 Effective Use of Technology in the Classroom

Relevant Bulletin Boards

The prescription of the bulletin board is typically twofold. One is to have a bulletin board that is connected to the lesson or content that is currently being covered. The other is to have a bulletin board that relates to the overall theme of the lesson. After those two, the range of bulletin boards is wide and open. Youth culture is an important responsive key here and an easy way to draw in students.

Fig. 7.4 Example of an Effective Bulletin Board

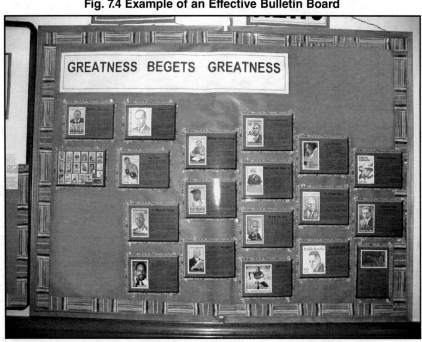

Displayed Student Work and Images of Students

CLR promotes student work everywhere. The recommendation at CLAS is that student work should be exchanged every three weeks. The work should be exemplary in nature but not exclusionary. We all recall the warm feeling that goes with seeing your work displayed; it is the classroom's version of having your name in lights. We want all students to have that feeling. There are some students who may not for whatever reason reach exemplary, so displaying students' work in a way that highlights the less-than-exemplary levels is key as well.

Fig. 7.5 Displaying Student Work

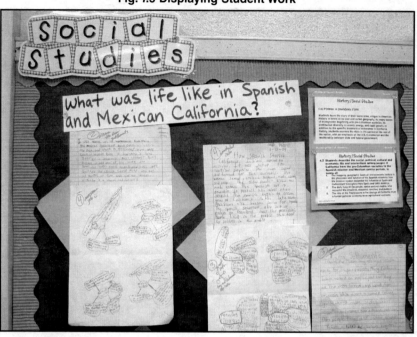

Examining the Learning Environment

Classroom walk-throughs are intended to provide a picture of learning in schools. They are "powerful tools that educators can use to stimulate conversations around improving teaching and learning" (Perry, cited in Richardson 2006, 2). At CLAS, we have walk-throughs so teachers can gain feedback from their colleagues.

Supporting that obvious purpose, as teachers visit other classrooms, they gain ideas about how to make their room more culturally responsive. We use the CLR Learning Environment Survey, a tool that helps us to focus our observations and follow-up conversations with colleagues. The survey topics include print-rich environment, learning centers, culturally colorful design, optimally arranged room arrangement, multiple libraries, technology, and relevant bulletin boards. Each topic is accompanied by a five-point rating scale ranging from very responsive to least responsive. The survey is in the section titled Resources for Teachers (Appendix G).

Fig. 7.6 Example of an Effective Learning Environment

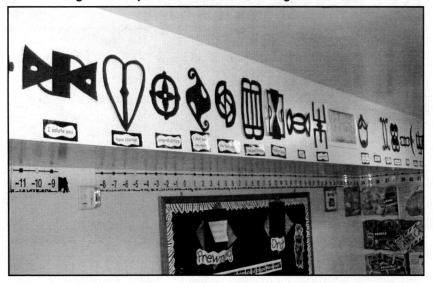

Summary

As you see from the principles presented in this chapter, the impact of the learning environment is about making positive first impressions with the students when they walk into the room in August or September. Several elements constitute an exemplary CLR learning environment, or what we at CLAS call the *recipe of success*. What must be remembered is that there is always room for teacher innovation in creating a learning environment that is responsive to the students' cultural and linguistic needs and expectations. Creating a responsive learning environment takes into consideration both physical and social factors. The physical factors include elements that make the classroom intellectually attractive and stimulating to students: furnishings and their arrangement, learning resources and their organization, displays of student work, and displays of items that reflect who the students are. Social considerations are also important in creating a positive learning climate: fair and clear procedures for classroom behavior, teacher use of fair and equitable strategies that support student learning, and activities that foster communication and self-sufficiency.

Reflection Guide

Think back to your responses to the statements in the Anticipation Guide at the beginning of the chapter. Have your responses changed as a result of what you read in the chapter? What new insights did you gain from the chapter?

_____ The traditional classroom structure with students sitting in rows is most effective in maintaining discipline with underserved students.

_____ Excessive use of decorative materials in the classroom can be distracting for underserved students.

_____ An inviting classroom environment encourages students to interact positively with one another and the teacher.

_____ Learning centers are necessary in primary-grade classrooms but are not essential for students in the upper grades, notably middle and secondary levels.

_____ Fair and clear procedures for classroom behaviors contribute to a sense of community in the classroom.

_____ A combination of teacher-directed and student-centered activities is needed to maintain a responsive learning environment.

1. Review the photographs showing features of classrooms at CLAS. Compare the features of your classroom to those of CLAS. What do you observe about similarities and differences?

2. Sometimes it is difficult for teachers to make changes in

the physical arrangement of the classroom. What, if any, difficulties have you encountered when you attempted to make such changes? How have you dealt with those problems?

3. With a colleague, use the CLR Learning Environment Survey (Appendix G) to examine your classrooms. Where are the strengths and limitations of your learning environment? What changes are necessary? What is your plan for making those changes?

Protocols for Increasing Student Engagement

Protocol: Let Me Hear You

Description: Students actively respond in unison to speaker either verbally or with movement (or both) to either an improvised or pretaught "call."

Why use it:	It is best to use this when:
• To actively engage all students • To validate and affirm culturally different forms of discourse, particularly as an aspect of codeswitching	• Getting students' attention • Transitioning between activities • Showing appreciation or acknowledgement

Protocol: Pick-a-Stick

Description: After the teacher poses a question, students think about the answer silently. After sufficient thought time, the teacher picks from a group of sticks that represent each student. The chosen student answers the question. Stick selection can continue until a sufficient number of answers are heard.

Why use it:	It is best to use this when:
• To hold all students accountable for participation through nonvolunteerism	• Randomly sampling students to assess prior knowledge • Randomly selecting students to assess understanding • Maintaining whole-group engagement during direct instruction

Protocol: Roll 'Em

Description: Students are divided in groups of 4–6. Students think about a posed question as the teacher rolls two number cubes. One number cube represents the table/group number and the other number cube represents the seat number. The student sitting in the seat represented by the rolled number cube answers the question. Rolling of the number cube can continue until a sufficient number of answers are heard.

Why use it:	It is best to use this when:
• To hold all students accountable for participation through nonvolunteerism	• Randomly sampling students to assess prior knowledge • Randomly selecting students to assess understanding • Maintaining whole-group engagement during direct instruction

Protocol: My Turn, Your Turn

Description: This turn-taking protocol is utilized in several protocols for participation and discussion. It is an explicit way of indicating when "jumping in" is not appropriate and reminds students that their turn to talk and ask questions will follow soon. In elementary classrooms, the teacher may remind students about the actions of good listeners with the phrase *Hands free, eyes on me, and voices off.*

Why use it:	It is best to use this when:
• To practice explicit turn taking, particularly as an aspect of codeswitching • Helps students practice turn taking without jumping in when they feel engaged	• It is important for one speaker to be heard, such as during direct instruction, presentations, guest speakers, etc.

Protocol: Give a Shout Out

Description: Students softly shout out responses at the same time. The teacher can record shout-outs on the board, if appropriate. Posed questions can require either one correct answer or a variety of short answers.

Why use it:	It is best to use this when:
• To actively engage all students • To validate and affirm culturally different forms of discourse, particularly as an aspect of codeswitching	• Checking for understanding on short 1–2 word answers (e.g., multiplication facts, brainstorming short 1–2 words) • Checking responses (such as synonyms with the Personal Thesaurus)

Protocol: Moment of Silence

Description: This is an explicit time for total silence, including on the part of the teacher.

Why use it:	It is best to use this when:
• To practice explicit silent work, particularly as an aspect of codeswitching	• Students are taking tests, quizzes, or completing independent assessments • Students are journal writing or completing quick writes • Students are in sustained silent reading (SSR) • Students are meditating or reflecting

Protocol: Train or Pass It On

Description: Students call on one another to answer and/or ask questions. Students should not raise their hands to be called on and should be encouraged to call on a variety of people in the classroom. Students can also "pass" on a question they do not want to answer by calling on another student for help. This is called "Pass It On." This can also be done with the use of a small soft object that students can toss to one another in order to "pass it on."

Why use it:	It is best to use this when:
• To hold all students accountable for participation through nonvolunteerism • To validate and affirm culturally different forms of discourse, particularly as an aspect of codeswitching • To provide for improvisation and variety • To provide an opportunity for students to control participation	• Checking for understanding, individually or collectively • A student has been selected via another protocol but needs assistance

Protocol: Raise a Righteous Hand

Description: Students raise a hand/fist to volunteer information that is specific to their experiences.

Why use it:	It is best to use this when:
• To practice explicit turn taking, particularly as an aspect of codeswitching	• Taking a poll or a vote • Eliciting very specific information from select individuals with particular experiences

Protocol: Whip Around

Description: Each student in the room takes a turn responding with quick answers to a posed question. The order should be based on seating in order for the teacher to avoid having to constantly facilitate the direction of the students answering. This should go very quickly around the room, so the question needs to be appropriately precise as well.

Why use it:	It is best to use this when:
• To practice explicit turn taking, particularly as an aspect of codeswitching • To validate everyone's responses • To practice precise, focused responses	• Checking whole-group understanding after a reading selection, directed instruction, or presentation • Needing brief, quick responses from all students

Protocol: Numbered Heads Together

Description: Students are divided in groups of 4–6 and numbered. When asked a question, they work together to find the best answer. When called together again, the teacher rolls a number cube and asks the students from each group with the number rolled to stand (e.g., "All 3s from each group, please stand."). Each student then represents the group and reports its answer.

Why use it:	It is best to use this when:
• To form a consensus and have everyone be accountable for the information	• Forming groups, such as for academic games • Reviewing information • Forming cooperative groups randomly

Protocol: Think-Pair-Share

Description: This involves a three-step cooperative structure. During the first step, students *think* silently about a question posed by the teacher. Individuals then *pair* up during the second step and exchange thoughts. In the third step, the pairs *share* their responses with other pairs or the entire group. It is a usually a good idea to have the individuals asked to share with the whole group to explain what their partner said in order to promote good listening skills.

Why use it:	It is best to use this when:
• To quickly clarify or share ideas about a topic/concept; to provide everyone with some talk time when there is a strong desire to share	• Accessing prior knowledge • Having all students share journal responses • Reviewing/summarizing information randomly

Protocol: Merry-Go-Round

Description: Each student takes a quick turn sharing with the team a thought or reaction to something posed by the teacher. Responses should be quick 1–5 word phrases in order to keep it going quickly and keep thoughts concise.

Why use it:	It is best to use this when:
• To share personal responses in a short time period without recording on paper	• Responding to literature • Having students express their strengths and needs while in a small group

Protocol: Put Your Two Cents In

Description: Each student has two cowry shells to use as talking pieces. In groups of four, each student takes a turn by putting one cowry shell in the center of the table and sharing his or her idea. When everyone has shared once, each student then puts one more cowry shell in at a time and responds to what someone else in the group has shared, e.g., "I agree with____ because…," or "I don't agree with _____ because…"

Why use it:	It is best to use this when:
• To share, question, and support opinions	• Discussing current events • Sharing opinions on topics • Giving ideas on a group assignment

Protocol: **Circle the Sage**

Description: The teacher polls the class to see which students have special knowledge to share (e.g., homework, understanding of long division). Then, those students (the sages) stand and spread out in the room. The teacher then has the rest of the classmates go to one of the sages, with no two members of the same team going to the same sage. The sage explains what he or she knows while the classmates listen, ask questions, and take notes. All students then return to their teams. Each in turn explains what he or she learned. Because most have gone to different sages, they compare notes. If there is a disagreement, they stand up as a team. Finally, the disagreements are aired and resolved.

Why use it:	**It is best to use this when:**
• To utilize the expertise of class members to share/teach others	• Sharing cultural traditions • Having students who understood a particular problem explain it to a small group • Having students share specific knowledge/understandings they may individually have

Protocol: **Give One, Get One**

Description: After thinking or journaling about a topic, students are asked to get up and find someone across the room with whom to share their thoughts or answers. Students are thus receiving an idea in exchange for giving one.

Why use it:	**It is best to use this when:**
• To have students choose with whom they would like to share • To allow movement	• Reviewing, summarizing, or clarifying information • Accessing prior knowledge

Protocol: Three-Step Interview

Description: Each member of a team chooses another member to be a partner. During the first step, individuals interview their partners by asking clarifying or interview questions. During the second step, partners reverse the roles. For the final step, members share their partner's response with the team.

Why use it:	It is best to use this when:
• To have students ask and answer student-created questions	• Needing an icebreaker • Students are working in groups, each with an assigned role • Conducting character interviews

Protocol: Jigsaw

Description: Groups of 4–5 students are established. Each group member is assigned some unique material to learn and then teach to his or her group members. To help in the learning, students across the class focusing on the same material get together to decide what is important and how to teach it. After practice in these "expert" groups, the original groups reform and students teach one another. Tests or assessments can follow.

Why use it:	It is best to use this when:
• To provide for interdependency and accountability within a small group	• Breaking up a reading selection or research topic into smaller parts for groups to share out

Protocol: Team-Pair-Solo

Description: Students do problems first as a team, then with a partner, and finally on their own.

Why use it:	It is best to use this when:
• To scaffold learning • Motivates students to tackle and succeed at problems that may be initially beyond their ability	• Reviewing content and skills • Researching information • Practicing a particular skill (such as order of operations)

Protocol: Partners

Description: The class is divided into teams of four. Half of each team is given an assignment to master to be able to teach the other half. Partners studying the same material go to one side of the room and consult with one another about the material and how to best teach it to the other half of their team. Teams then go back together, with each set of partners teaching the other set. Partners quiz and tutor their teammates. The team reviews how well they learned and taught and how they might improve the process.

Why use it:	It is best to use this when:
• To provide for interdependency and accountability within a small group	• Reviewing content and skills • Researching information • Practicing a particular skill (such as order of operations)

Protocol: Corners

Description: Each student moves to a corner of the room that represents a teacher-determined alternative or point on a scale. Students discuss their choices in their own corners and then listen to and paraphrase or debate ideas and opinions from other corners.

Why use it:	It is best to use this when:
• To develop student-choice interest groups • To establish and support opinions	• Having students indicate which character they associate with in a story • Having students indicate preferences, hobbies, or experiences • Having students show where they stand on an issue • Forming groups around common interests or specific skills

Protocol: **Send-a-Problem**

Description: Each student writes a review problem on a flash card and asks teammates to answer or solve it. Review questions are passed to another group to be answered.

Why use it:	It is best to use this when:
• To ask and answer student-created questions	• Discussing and reviewing material or potential solutions to problems related to content information

Protocol: **Silent Appointment**

Description: After the teacher poses a problem/question to be discussed, students make "silent appointments" with each other by making eye contact and nodding to indicate that an appointment has been made. Students then go to their appointments and share. The teacher should then review with the whole class by asking what students heard that was shared by others.

Why use it:	It is best to use this when:
• To have students choose with whom they would like to share; to allow movement	• Reviewing, summarizing, or clarifying information • Sharing prior knowledge • Having students share journal responses

Protocol: **Musical Shares**

Description: This is similar to Give One, Get One. The teacher poses a question and turns on music. Students move/dance around the classroom until the music is turned off. Students discuss the question with whomever they are closest to when the music is turned off. The teacher resumes music and the process continues until they have had enough opportunities to share.

Why use it:	It is best to use this when:
• To incorporate music and movement with opportunities to share ideas	• Reviewing, summarizing, or clarifying information • Sharing prior knowledge • Having students share journal responses

Protocol: Roundtable

Description: Each team uses a single sheet of paper and pencil and, in turn, responds to a question or problem by stating their ideas aloud as they write them on the paper. The paper is then passed around the table until time is called. It is important that the ideas be vocalized for several reasons: Silence in a setting like this is boring, rather than golden; other team members need to be reflecting on the proffered thoughts; variety results because teammates learn immediately that someone has come up with an idea that they know now not to repeat; and hearing the responses said aloud means that students do not have to waste valuable brainstorming time by reading the previous ideas on the page. Team members are encouraged not to skip turns, but if their thoughts are at a standstill, they are allowed to say "Pass" rather than turn the brainstorm into a brain drizzle. Thus, there is almost universal participation in Roundtable.

Why use it:	It is best to use this when:
• To have all students write and contribute to a group's ideas	• Brainstorming ideas on a topic • Generating a large number of responses to a single question or group of questions

Protocol: Inner-Outer Circle

Description: There should be two circles, with the outer-circle students facing inward and the inner circle students facing outward. Students in the outer circle begin by asking the student facing them on the inner circle a question. This question may be prepared by either the students themselves or the teacher. Once the inner-circle student has had an opportunity to answer, either the outer or inner circle rotates and the process is repeated until a full rotation is made. Then, the inner circle has the opportunity to ask questions as the outer circle responds, and so forth.

Why use it:	It is best to use this when:
• To allow a variety of questions and interactions in a short time span while including the use of movement	• Reviewing for an assessment • Practicing questioning and responding • Checking for comprehension of a reading passage

Protocol: Round-Robin Brainstorming

Description: One person in each team is appointed as the recorder. An open-ended question is posed and students are given time to think about answers. After the think time, members of the team share responses with one another round-robin style. The recorder writes down the answers of the group members. The person next to the recorder starts, and each person in the group gives an answer in order until time is called. A person may "pass," if needed, and provide input on the next rotation after he or she has had time to think.

Why use it:	It is best to use this when:
• To allow a proficient writer to do all the writing while others share verbally	• Brainstorming ideas on a topic • Generating a large number of response to a single question or group of questions

Protocol: Greet and Respond/Tea Party

Description: Provide each student with an unfinished sentence, question, or prompt to which a response can be made. As the teacher calls out or displays particular settings/situations, students walk around and use appropriate greetings to greet each other, read their prompts, and respond to each other in turn.

Why use it:	It is best to use this when:
• To allow a variety of questions and interactions in a short time span while allowing movement	• Previewing literature or other content by accessing or introducing prior knowledge • Reviewing learning • Checking for comprehension • Practicing questioning and responding • Practicing explicit situational appropriateness

Examples of Effective Attention Signals

Name: Voice Check

Description: Voice Check is used to change the volume of the student voices in the classroom.

How-to Steps:

Teacher says, "Voice Check" in the tone and level of volume in which he or she wants the students to respond. Students respond, "1-2, 1-2."

Name: Holla Back

Description: Teacher calls out a phrase from a popular song and the students respond with the second word.

How-to Steps:

Teacher says, "Holla." Students respond, "Back."

Name: Student Call

Description: Teacher calls the name of the class and the students respond with "Woo! Woo!" or "That's Who We Are."

How-to Steps:

Teacher and class decide on the response together to gain buy-in. This can also be done with school names and mascots.

Name: When I Move, You Move

Description: This can be used as a transition for students who are getting materials out or going to another place in the classroom.

How-to Steps:

Teacher calls or raps, "When I Move, You Move," and the students call back, "Just like that."

Name: When I Say...

Description: Teacher gives direction during the call-and-response.

How-to Steps:

Teacher says, "When I say *peace*, you say *quiet*."

Teacher: Peace

Students: Quiet

Name: West African Chant

Description: This is derived from the West African language in which the teacher asks the students if they are ready to learn by paying attention. If students respond with yes, then they are ready and listening.

How-to Steps:

Teacher says, "Ah-go" (pay attention), and students reply, "Ah-may" (we are listening).

Name: Teacher Chant 1

Description: This is a longer call-and-response attention getter for those classrooms that have students who need more time to focus back on the teacher. Therefore, by chanting back, they know that they have a few more seconds before full attention is needed.

How-to Steps:

Teacher begins and students reply the following:

Teacher: One, two

Students: Eyes on you.

Teacher: Three, four

Students: I talk no more.

Teacher: Five, six

Students: We play no tricks.

Teacher: Seven, eight

Students: Sit up straight.

Teacher: Nine, ten

Students: We're ready to begin.

Name: Teacher Chant 2

Description: This is a longer call-and-response attention getter for those classrooms that have students who need more time to focus back on the teacher. Therefore, by chanting back, they know that they have a few more seconds before full attention is needed.

How-to Steps:

Teacher begins and students reply the following:

Teacher: One, two, three—eyes on ME!

Students: One, two—eyes on YOU!

Name: Teacher Chant 3

Description: This is a longer call-and-response attention getter for those classrooms that have students who need more time to focus back on the teacher. Therefore, by chanting back, they know that they have a few more seconds before full attention is needed.

How-to Steps:

Teacher begins and students reply the following:

Teacher: All set?

Students: You bet!

Name: Catch the Beat

Description: Teacher snaps and/or claps out a rhythm. Students respond back with the same rhythm. This calls for students to have their hands free to "catch the beat," which means that they will not continue writing, cutting, or pasting while responding, as their hands are free of all items.

How-to Steps:

Catch the Beat changes every time so that students are not set to the same rhythm.

Teacher: (*Claps three times*)

Students: (*Claps three times*)

Teacher: (*Clap, snap, clap*)

Students: (*Clap, snap, clap*)

Name: Give Me Five

Description: This call-and-response calls for students to have hands free while responding to the teacher.

How-to Steps:

The teacher raises a hand, and the students raise their hands back to the teacher and give a five in the air. The teacher can then ask students to give a five to one another.

Name: Give Yourself Some Love

Description: This is used when students should be acknowledged for these successes as a whole group.

How-to Steps:

The teacher tells the students, "Hands up, hand down, hands out, hands in, now give yourself some love." The students wrap their arms around themselves and hug themselves.

Name: Variation of Head, Shoulder, Knees, and Toes

Description: When students are restless, the teacher tells students to touch body parts at varying speeds.

How-to Steps:

The teacher says in a singing voice, "Hands on your head, hands on your knees, hands on your elbows, (the teacher speeds up the pace), on cheeks, on your nose, on your tummy, (the teacher slows the pace down or goes even faster) hands on your chin, hands on your forehead, hands on your shoulders, on your mouth, eyes, and toes."

Name: Brain Break

Description: When students are restless, moving around, or talkative, the teacher calls out, "Brain Break."

How-to Steps:

After the teacher calls a "brain break," he or she leads the class in various activities such as yoga stretches or breathing.

Culturally Responsive Books

African American Emphasis

Grades K–2

Allen, Debbie and Nelson, Kadir. 2003. *Dancing in the Wings.* London: Puffin Books.

Angelou, Maya. 1993. *Life Doesn't Frighten Me.* New York: Stewart, Tabori, and Chang.

Asare, Meshack. 1997. *Sosu's Call.* San Diego, CA: Kane/Miller Book Publishers.

Barnwell, Ysaye. 2000. *Um Hmm: African American Tales (Secrets of the World).* Boulder, CO: Sounds True Books.

Bearden, Romare. 2003. *Li'l Dan the Drummer Boy: A Civil War Story.* New York: Simon and Schuster Children's Publishing.

Brown, M. W. 2000. *A Baby is Born.* New York: Hyperion Books.

Bryan, Ashley. 2003. *Beautiful Blackbird.* New York: Atheneum Books for Young Readers.

Burleigh, Robert. 2004. *Langston's Train Ride.* New York: Scholastic, Inc.

Byrd, Donald. 2001. *The Harlem Nutcracker: Based on the Ballet.* New York: Hyperion Books for Children.

Carney-Nunes, Charisse and Williams, Ann Marie. 2007. *I Dream for You a World: A Covenant for Our Children.* Washington, D.C.: Brand Nu Words.

Coleman, Evelyn. 1998. *To be a Drum.* Park Ridge, IL: Albert Whitman & Company.

Cook, Michelle. 2009. *Our Children Can Soar: A Celebration of Rosa, Barack, and the Pioneers of Change.* New York: Bloomsbury USA.

Cosby, Bill. 2003. *Friends of a Feather: One of Life's Little Fables.* New York: HarperCollins.

Cunnane, Kelly. and Juan, Ana. 2006. *For You are a Kenyan Child.* New York: Atheneum Books for Young Readers.

Daly, Niki. 2002. *What's Cooking, Jamela?.* London: Frances Lincoln Ltd.

———. 2005. *Where's Jamela?* London: Frances Lincoln Ltd.

Dillon, Leo. and Dillon, Dillon. 2007. *Jazz on a Saturday Night.* New York: Blue Sky Press.

Duggleby, John. 1998. *Story Painter: The Life of Jacob Lawrence.* San Francisco, CA: Chronicle Books.

Ehrhardt, Karen. 2006. *This Jazz Man.* Chicago: Houghton Mifflin Harcourt.

Evans, Shane. 2003. *Homemade Love.* New York: Hyperion Books for Children.

Greenfield, Eloise. 2006. *The Friendly Four.* New York: HarperCollins.

Hartfield, Claire. 2002. *Me and Uncle Romie: A Story Inspired by the Life and Art of Romare Bearden.* New York: Dial Books for Young Readers.

Higginsen, Vy. 1995. *This Is My Song: A Collection of Gospel Music for the Family.* New York: Crown Publishing Group.

Holiday, Billie. and Herzog, A. 2007. *God Bless the Child.* New York: HarperCollins.

Hooks, Bell. 2004. *Skin Again.* New York: Hyperion Books for Children.

Hughes, Langston. 2009. *My People.* New York: Atheneum Books for Young Readers.

Hurston, Zora Neale. 2004. *What's the Hurry Fox?: And Other Animal Stories.* New York: HarperCollins.

Hurston, Zura Neale and Thomas, Joyce Carol. 2005. *The Six Fools.* New York: HarperCollins.

Jackson, Ellen. 2005. *Earth Mother.* New York: Bloomsbury USA.

Johnson, Angela. 2007. *Lily Brown's Paintings.* London: Orchard Books.

Johnson, James Weldon. 2000. *Lift Every Voice and Sing: Selected Poems.* New York: Penguin.

Jordan, Deloris and Jordan, Roslyn. 2004. *Did I Tell You I Love You Today?* New York: Simon and Schuster Books for Young Readers.

Lee, Spike and Lee, Tonya 2007. *Please, Baby, Please.* New York: Simon and Schuster Children's Publishing.

———. 2009. *Please, Puppy, Please.* New York: Simon and Schuster Children's Publishing.

Lessac, Frané. 2005. *Island Counting 1 2 3.* Somerville, MA: Candlewick Press.

Levine, Ellen and Nelson, Kadir. 2007. *Henry's Freedom Box.* New York: Scholastic Press.

Livingston, Maya Cohn. 1992. *Let Freedom Ring: A Ballad of Martin Luther King, Jr.* New York: Holiday House.

Lyons, Mary. 2005. *Roy Makes a Car.* New York: Atheneum Books for Young Readers.

McGill, Alice. 2000. *In the Hollow of Your Hand: Slave Lullabies.* Chicago: Houghton Mifflin Harcourt.

McKissack, Patricia. 2005. *Where Crocodiles Have Wings.* New York: Holiday House.

McKissack, Patricia and Moss, Onawuni Jean. 2005. *Precious and the Boo Hag.* New York: Simon and Schuster Children's Publishing.

Nelson, Kadir. 2005. *He's Got the Whole World in His Hands.* New York: Dial Press for Young Readers,

Nolen, Jerdine. 2005. *Hewitt Anderson's Great Big Life.* New York: Simon and Schuster Books for Young Readers.

Norman, Lissette. 2006. *My Feet are Laughing.* New York: Farrar Straus Giroux.

Otto, Carolyn. 2008. *Celebrate Kwanzaa.* Margate, FL: National Geographic Books.

Pinkney, Andrea Davis. 2003. *Fishing Day.* New York: Hyperion Books for Children.

———. 2004. *Sleeping Cutie.* Chicago: Houghton Mifflin Harcourt.

Rappaport, Doreen. 2008. *Martin's Big Words: The Life of Dr. Martin Luther King, Jr.* Pittsburg, CA: Paw Prints Press.

Shange, Ntozake. 1994. *I Live in Music: Poem.* New York: Stewart, Tabori, and Chang.

Shange, Ntozake and Nelson, Kadir. 2009. *Coretta Scott.* New York: HarperCollins.

Siegelson, Kim. 1999. *In the Time of the Drums.* New York: Hyperion Books for Children.

Smalls, Irene. 2005. *My Nana and Me.* New York: Hachette Digital, Inc.

Stroud, Bettye. 2005. *The Patchwork Path: A Quilt Map to Freedom.* Somerville, MA: Candlewick Press.

Taylor, Debbie. 2004. *Sweet Music in Harlem.* New York: Lee and Low Books.

Thomas, Garen Eileen. 2004. *Santa's Kwanzaa.* New York: Hyperion Books for Children.

Turner-Denstaedt, Melanie. 2009. *The Hat That Clara B. Wore.* New York: Farrar Straus Giroux.

Weatherford, Carole Boston. 2008. *Moses: When Harriet Tubman Led Her People to Freedom.* Pittsburgh, CA: Paw Prints Press.

Weinstein, Muriel Harris. 2008. *When Louis Armstrong Taught Me Scat.* San Francisco, CA: Chronicle Books.

Grades 3–5

Adler, David. 2005. *Joe Louis: America's Fighter.* Chicago: Houghton Mifflin Harcourt.

Aston, Dianna Hutts. 2008. *The Moon Over Star.* New York: Dial Books for Young Readers.

Barber, Ronde. 2005. *By My Brother's Side.* New York: Scholastic, Inc.

Berlin, Ira. 1998. *Many Thousands Gone: The First Two Centuries of Slavery in North America.* Cambridge, MA: Harvard University Press.

Burns, Khepra. 2001. *Mansa Musa: The Lion of Mali.* Chicago: Houghton Mifflin Harcourt.

Burns, Khepra and Miles, William. 1995. *Black Stars in Orbit: NASA's African-American Astronauts.* Chicago: Harcourt Brace and Co.

Clinton, Catherine. 2007. *When Harriet Met Sojourner.* New York: HarperCollins.

Dungy, Tony. 2008. *You Can Do It!* New York: Simon and Schuster Children's Publishing.

Ellis, Carl. 1996. *Free at Last? The Gospel in the African-American Experience.* Downer's Grove, IL: InterVarsity Press.

Elster, Jean Alicia. 2002. *I Have a Dream, Too!* Valley Forge, PA: Judson Press.

Elster, Jean Alicia. 2002. *I'll Fly My Own Plane.* Valley Forge, PA: Judson Press.

Frazier, Sundee. 2008. *Brendan Buckley's Universe and Everything in It.* New York: Random House Digital, Inc.

Giovanni, Nikki. 2008. *Lincoln and Douglass: An American Friendship.* New York: Henry Holt Books for Young Readers.

Gladstone, Valerie. 2009. *A Young Dancer: The Life of an Ailey Student.* New York: Macmillan.

Golenbock, Peter. 1992. *Teammates.* Chicago: Houghton Mifflin Harcourt.

Grimes, Nikki and Collier, Bryan. 2008. *Barack Obama: Son of Promise, Child of Hope.* New York: Simon & Schuster Books for Young Readers.

Hamilton, Virginia. 2004. *The People Could Fly*. New York: A. A. Knopf.

Haskins, Jim. and Benson, Kathleen. 2006. *John Lewis in the Lead: A Story of the Civil Rights Movement*. New York: Lee & Low.

Johnson, Angela. 2007. *Wind Flyers*. New York: Simon and Schuster.

Jordan, Deloris. and Jordan, Roslyn. 2007. *Michael's Golden Rules*. New York: Simon and Schuster.

King Farris, Christine. 2008. *March On! The Day My Brother Martin Changed the World*. New York: Scholastic, Inc.

———. 2009. *My Brother Martin: A Sister Remembers Growing Up with the Rev. Dr. Martin Luther King Jr.* Charlotte, NC: Baker and Taylor.

Marsalis, Wynton and Schaap, Phil. 2007. *Jazz ABZ: An A to Z Collection of Jazz Portraits with Art Print*. Somerville, MA: Candlewick Press.

McKissack, Patricia. 2007. *All-I-Ever-Want Christmas Doll*. New York: Schwartz & Wade Books.

McKissack, Patricia and Cabrera, Cozbi. 2008. *Stitchin' and Pullin': A Gee's Bend Quilt*. New York: Random House Children's Books.

McKissack, Patricia and Zarembaka, Arlene. 2004. *To Establish Justice: Citizenship and the Constitution*. New York: Random House Children's Books.

Michelson, Richard. 2008. *As Good as Anybody: Martin Luther King, Jr. and Abraham Joshua Heschel's Amazing March toward Freedom*. New York: A.A. Knopf.

Myers, Walter Dean. 2004. *Here in Harlem: Poems in Many Voices*. New York: Holiday House.

Negron, Ray. 2008. *The Greatest Story Never Told*. New York: HarperCollins.

Nelson, Kadir. 2008. *We Are the Ship: The Story of Negro League Baseball*. New York: Hyperion Books for Children.

Nelson, Kadir and D. Rappaport. 2008. *Abe's Honest Words: The Life of Abraham Lincoln*. New York: Hyperion Books for Children.

Nelson, Marilyn. and Kuklin, Susan. 2009. *Beautiful Ballerina.* New York: Scholastic, Inc.

Nelson, Vaundas Micheaux. 2009. *Bad News for Outlaws: The Remarkable Life of Bass Reeves, Deputy of U.S. Marshal.* Minneapolis, MN: Carolrhoda Books.

Price, Leontyne. 1997. *Aida.* London: Sandpiper.

Rappaport, Doreen. 2001. *No More!: Stories and Songs of Slave Resistance.* Somerville, MA: Candlewick Press.

Rappaport, Doreen. 2006. *Nobody Gonna Turn Me 'Round: Stories and Songs of the Civil Rights Movement.* Somerville, MA: Candlewick Press.

Rockwell, Anne and Christie, R. Gregory. 2002. *Only Passing through.* New York: Random House Children's Books.

Root, B. 2006. *Game Day.* New York: Scholastic, Inc.

Ryan, Pam Munoz. 2002. *When Marian Sang: The True Recital of Marian Anderson: The Voice of a Century.* New York: Scholastic Press.

Shange, Ntozake. 2004. *Ellington Was Not a Street.* New York: Simon and Schuster Books for Young Readers.

Smith Jr., Charles. R. and Smith, C. 2010. *Twelve Rounds to Glory: The Story of Muhammad Ali.* Eastsound, WA: Turtleback Books.

Turner, Glennette Tilley. 2006. *An Apple for Harriet Tubman.* Chicago, IL: Albert Whitman and Company.

Weatherford, Carol Boston. 2007. *I, Matthew Henson: Polar Explorer.* New York: Bloomsbury Publishing USA.

Whelan, Gloria. 2005. *Friend on Freedom River.* Farmington Hills, MI: Sleeping Bear Press.

Williams-Garcia, Rita. 2010. *One Crazy Summer.* New York: HarperCollins.

Williams, Mary. 2005. *Brothers in Hope: The Story of the Lost Boys of Sudan.* New York: Lee and Low Books.

Williams, Sherley Anne. 1997. *Working cotton.* Chicago: Houghton Mifflin Harcourt.

Abdul-Jabbar, K. and Steinberg, A. 2000. *Black Profiles in Courage: A Legacy of African American Achievement.* New York: HarperCollins.

Adoff, Jaime. 2009. *The Death of Jayson Porter.* New York: Hyperion Books.

Bennett Jr., Lerone. 2007. *Forced Into Glory: Abraham Lincoln's White Dream.* Chicago, Johnson Publishing Company.

Blackmon, Douglas A. 2009. *Slavery by Another Name: The Re-Enslavement of Black Americans from the Civil War to World War II.* New York: Random House Digital, Inc.

Bolden, Tonya. 2004. *Wake Up Our Souls: A Celebration of Black American Artists.* New York: H. N. Abrams.

———. 2007. M.L.K.: *Journey of a King.* New York: Abrams Books for Young Readers.

Boyd, Herb. 2000. *Autobiography of a People: Three Centuries of African American History Told by Those Who Lived It.* New York: Random House Digital, Inc.

Brown, Cupcake. 2006. *A Piece of Cake: A memoir.* New York: Random House Digital, Inc.

Burns, Kephra and Miles, William. 1995. *Black Stars in Orbit: NASA's African-American Astronauts.* Chicago: Harcourt Brace and Co.

Chin-Lee, Cynthia. 2010. *Amelia to Zora: Twenty-Six Women Who Changed the World.* Watertown, MA: Charlesbridge Publishing.

Crisler, Curtis L. and Cooper, Floyd. 2007. *Tough Boy Sonatas.* Honesdale, PA: Boyds Mills Press.

Curtis, Christopher Paul. 2006. *Bucking the Sarge.* New York: Random House Digital, Inc.

———. 2009. *Elijah of Buxton.* Eastsound, WA: Turtleback Books.

Gourse, Leslie. 2007. *Sophisticated Ladies: The Great Women of Jazz.* London: Penguin Young Readers Group.

Greenfield, Eloise. 2003. *How they Got Over: African Americans and the Call of the Sea.* New York: HarperCollins.

Hamilton, Virginia. 2002. *Time Pieces: The Book of Times.* New York: Scholastic Inc.

Harper, Hill. 2007. *Letters to a Young Brother: Manifest Your Destiny.* London: Penguin Books.

———. 2009. *Letters to a Young Sister: Define Your Destiny.* London: Penguin Books.

Hine, Darlene Clark. and Thompson, Kathleen. 1999. *A Shining Thread of Hope: The History of Black Women in America.* New York: Random House Digital.

Hughes, Langston, Hubbard, D., Johnson, D., McLaren, J., and Miller, B. R. 2001. *The Collected Works of Langston Hughes.* Columbia, MO: University of Missouri Press.

Jackson, David. 2011. *Up from Here.* Raleigh, NC: Lulu Publishing.

Mafundikwa, Saki. 2007. *Afrikan Alphabets: The Story of Writing in Afrika.* Brooklyn, NY: Mark Batty Publisher.

Massaquoi, Hans J. 2001. *Destined to Witness: Growing Up Black in Nazi Germany.* New York: HarperCollins.

McCormick, Patricia. 2006. *Sold.* New York: Hyperion Books.

McWhorter, Diane. 2004. *A Dream of Freedom: The Civil Rights Movement from 1954 to 1968.* New York: Scholastic Inc.

Meltzer, Milton. 2000. *There Comes a Time: The struggle for Civil Rights.* New York: Random House Digital Inc.

Mills, Kay. 2007. *This Little Light of Mine: The Life of Fannie Lou Hamer.* Baltimore, MD: University Press of Kentucky.

Morrison, Toni. 2007. *The Bluest Eye.* New York: Random House Digital Inc.

Myers, Walter Dean. 1996. *The Glory Field.* New York: Scholastic Inc.

———. 2007. *Harlem Summer.* New York: Scholastic Inc.

———. 2008. *The Beast.* Pittsburg, CA: Paw Prints.

Nelson, Kadir and Obama, B. 2009. *Change has Come: An Artist Celebrates our American Spirit.* New York: Simon and Schuster.

Pesci, David. 1997. *Amistad.* Cambridge, MA: Marlowe and Co.

Powell, Kevin. 2008. *The Black Male Handbook: A Blueprint for Life.* New York: Simon and Schuster.

Rolling, James Haywood Jr. 2005. *Come Look with Me: Discovering African American Art for Children.* West Palm Beach, FL: Lickle Publishing Inc.

Sutcliffe, Jane. 2007. *Marian Anderson.* Minneapolis, MN: Lerner Publishing Group.

Thomas, Joyce Carol. 2008. *Collected Novels for Teens: Bright shadow/Water girl/The golden pasture/Journey.* New York: Hyperion Books.

Vanzant, Iyanla. 1999. *Don't Give It Away!: A Workbook of Self-Awareness and Self-Affirmations for Young Women.* New York: Simon and Schuster.

X, Malcom. 2007. *Autobiography of Malcom X.* London: Penguin Books.

Latino Emphasis

Grades K–2

Alire-Sáenz, Benjamin. *A Gift from Papá Diego.* El Paso, TX: Cinco Punto Press.

Argueta, J. 2005. *Moony Luna: Luna, Lunita Lunera.* San Francisco, CA: Children's Book Press.

Caraballo, S. 2005. *My Parents: Heroes of the Harvest.* Houston, TX: Arte Publico Press.

Cisneros, Sandra. 1997. *Hairs/Pelitos.* Dragonfly Books.

Colon-Vila, L. 2009. *Salsa.* Houston, TX: Arte Publico Press.

Córdova, Amy. 2004. *The Santero's Miracle: A Bilingual Story.* Albuquerque, NM: University of New Mexico Press.

Costales, A. 2007. *Abuelita Full of Life.* Lanham, MD: Copper Square Publishing.

Cumpiano, I. 2005. *Quinito's Neighborhood.* San Francisco, CA: Children's Book Press.

De La Hoya, O. 2006. *Super Oscar.* New York: Simon and Schuster Children's Publishing.

Evans, S. W. 2003. *Homemade Love.* New York: Hyperion Books for Children.

Geeslin, C. 2004. *Elena's Serenade.* New York: Simon and Schuster Children's Publishing.

Gonzales-Bertrand, Diane. 2003. *The Empanadas that Abuela Made.* Houston, TX: Piñata Books.

Lomas-Garza, Carmen. 2001. *In My Family.* San Francisco, CA: Children's Book Press.

Paulsen, G. 1998. *The Tortilla Factory.* Chicago: Houghton Mifflin Harcourt.

Shute, Linda. 1995. *Rabbit Wishes.* New York, NY: HarperCollins Publishers.

Soto, G. 2006. *My Little Car.* New York: Putnam Juvenile.

Soto, Gary. 1996. *Too Many Tamales.* New York, NY: Puffin Publishing.

Tenorio-Coscarelli, J. 2003. *The Burrito Boy.* Lake Elsinore, CA: Quarter Inch Publishing.

Winter, J. 2002. *Frida.* New York: Arthur A. Levine Books.

Grades 3–5

Alvarez, Julia. 2002. *How Tia Lola Came to Stay.* New York: Scholastic, Inc.

Argueta, J., Amado, E., and Calderón, G. 2003. *Zipitio.* Toronto, ON: Groundwood Books.

Atkin, S. B. 2001. *Voices from the fields: Children of Migrant Farmworkers Tell Their Stories.* New York: Scholastic Press.

Cameron, Ann. *The Most Beautiful Place in the World*. New York, NY: Yearling.

Cohn, D. 2005. *¡Sí se puede!/Yes we can!* El Paso, TX: Cinco Puntos Press.

Hayes, Joe. 2003. *The Day It Snowed Tortillas*. El Paso, TX: Cinco Puntos Press.

Jiménez, F. 2000. *La mariposa*. Chicago: Houghton Mifflin Harcourt.

Krull, K. 2003. *Harvesting Hope: The Story of Cesar Chavez*. Chicago: Harcourt Children's Books.

Laínez, R. C. 2004. *Waiting for Papa*. Houston, TX: Piñata Books.

Lomas-Garza, Carmen. *Family Pictures*. Logan, IA: Perfection Learning.

Mohr, Nicholasa. 1992. *All for the Better: A Story of El Barrio (Stories of America)*. Chicago: Houghton Mifflin Harcourt.

Palacios, Argentina. 1992. *Viva Mexico!: The Story of Benito Juarez and Cinco de Mayo*. Chicago: Houghton Mifflin Harcourt.

Perez, Amada Irma. I. 2007. *Nana's Big Surprises*. San Francisco, CA: Children's Book Press.

———. 2008. *My Very Own Room*. San Francisco CA: Children's Book Press.

———. 2009. *My Diary from Here to There*. San Francisco, CA: Children's Book Press.

Ray, D. K. 2006. *To Go Singing through the World: The Childhood of Pablo Neruda*. New York: Farrar Straus and Giroux.

Sasso, S. E. 2005. *Abuelita's Secret Matzahs*. Cincinnati, OH: Clerisy Press.

Serrano, F., Balch, T., Serrano, P., and Engelbert, J. 2007. *The Poet King of Tezcoco*. Toronto, ON: Groundwood Books.

Grades 6–12

Alvarez, Julia. 2002. *How Tia Lola Came to Stay*. New York: Scholastic, Inc.

Atkin, S. B. 2001. *Voices from the Fields: Children of Migrant Farmworkers Tell Their Stories*. New York: Scholastic Press.

Belpre, Pura. 1996. *Firefly Summer*. Houston, TX: Arte Publico Press

Charlton-Trujillo, E. E. 2007. *Prizefighter En Mi Casa*. New York: Random House Digital, Inc.

Cofer, J. O. 2006. *Call Me Maria*. New York: Scholastic Paperbacks.

Colin, J. J. 2008. *Cesar Chavez: The Struggle for Justice*. Houston, TX: Arte Publico Press.

Cruz, M. C. 2003. *Border Crossing*. Houston, TX: Piñata Books.

Délano, P., Monroy, M., Higgins, S. 2006. *When I Was a Boy Neruda Called Me Policarpo: A Memoir.* Toronto, ON: Groundwater Books.

Duncan, C. M. 2000. *Worlds apart: Why Poverty Persists in Rural America.* New Haven, CT: Yale University Press.

Griffin, P. R. 2002. *The Music Thief.* New York: Macmillan.

Herrera, Juan Felipe. 2005. *Downtown Boy*. New York: Scholastic, Inc.

López, L. 2006. *Call me Henri*. Willimantic, CT: Curbstone Press.

Osa, Nancy. 2005. *Cuba 15*. New York, NY: Delacorte Press Books for Young Readers.

Rhoads, Dorothy. 1993. *The Corn Grows Ripe*. New York, NY: Puffin Publications.

Soto, G. 2006. *Petty Crimes*. Chicago: Houghton Mifflin Harcourt.

Soto, G., and Dunnick, R. 2002. *Fearless Fernie*. New York: Putnam Juvenile.

Native American Emphasis

Grades K–2

Begay, Shonto. 1992. *Ma'ii and Cousin Horned Toad*. New York: Scholastic, Inc.

Bruchac, Joseph. 1993. *Fox Song*. New York: Bt Bound.

———. 1995. *Gluskabe and the Four Wishes*. New York, NY: Dutton Juvenille.

Crandell, Rachel. 2002. *Hands of the Maya: Villagers at Work and Play*. New York, NY: Holt & Co.

dePaola, Tomie. 1996. *The Legend of the Bluebonnet*. New York, NY: Puffin Publications.

———. 1996. *The Legend of the Indian Paintbrush*. New York, NY: Puffin Publications.

Goble, Paul. 1984. *The Gift of the Sacred Dog*. New York, NY: Aladdin Paperbacks.

———. 1993. *Beyond the Ridge*. New York, NY: Aladdin Paperbacks.

———. 1993. *Death of the Iron Horse*. New York, NY: Aladdin Paperbacks.

———. 1993. *The Girl Who Loved Wild Horses*. New York, NY: Aladdin Paperbacks.

Grossman, Virginia. 1995. *Ten Little Rabbits*. San Francisco, CA: Chronicle Books.

Larry, Charles. 1995. *Peboan and Seegwun*. Elgin, IL: Sunburst.

Lind, Michael. 2003. *Bluebonnet Girl*. New York, NY: Henry Holt & Co.

Martin, Bill. 1997. *Knots on a Counting Rope*. New York, NY: Henry Holt & Co.

Martin, Rafe. 1998. *The Rough-Face Girl*. New York, NY: Puffin Publications.

McDermott, Gerald. 1977. *Arrow to the Sun: A Pueblo Indian Tale*. New York, NY: Puffin Publications.

Pinola, Lanny. 1997. *Fire Race: A Karuk Coyote Tale of How Fire Came to the People*. San Francisco, CA: Chronicle Books.

Van Laan, Nancy. 1995. *In a Circle Long Ago: A Treasury of Native Lore from North America*. New York, NY: Knopf Books for Young Readers.

Grades 3–5

Ancona, George. 1995. *Earth Daughter: Alicia of Acoma Pueblo*. Chicago, IL: Simon and Schuster Books for Young Readers.

Bierhorst, John. 1995. *The White Deer and Other Stories Told by the Lenape*. New York: HarperCollins.

Bruchac, Joseph. 1998. *The Arrow Over the Door*. Dial Books for Young Readers. New York, NY: Penguin Group.

Cohlene, Terri. 1990. *Clamshell Boy: A Makah Legend*. Mahwah, NJ: Watermill Press.

———. 1996. *Little Firefly*. New York, NY: Troll Communications.

———. 1996. *Quillworker: Native American Legends*. New York, NY: Troll Communications.

———. 1996. *Turquoise Boy: Native American Legends*. New York, NY: Troll Communications.

———. 1997. *Ka Ha Si and the Loon: Native American Legends*. New York, NY: Troll Communications.

———. 1998. *Dancing Drum: Native American Legends*. New York, NY: Troll Communications.

Erdrich, Lise. 2003. *Sacagawea*. Minneapolis, MN: Carolrhoda Books, Inc.

Freedman, Russell. 1994. *An Indian Winter*. New York, NY: Holiday House.

Littlechild, George. 2003. *This Land Is My Land*. San Francisco, CA: Children's Book Press.

Loyie, Larry. 2005. *As Long as the Rivers Flow*. Toronto, ON: Groundwood Books.

Miles, Miska. 1985. *Annie and the Old One*. New York, NY: Little, Brown Books for Young Readers.

Rinaldi, Ann. *My Heart Is on the Ground: The Diary of Nannie Little Rose, a Sioux Girl*. New York: Scholastic Press.

Rose, LaVera. 2004. *Grandchildren of the Lakota*. Minneapolis, MN: Carolrhoda Books Inc.

Smith, Cynthia. 2004. *Indian Shoes*. New York, NY: HarperCollins Publishers.

Speare, Elizabeth George. 1984. *The Sign of the Beaver*. New York, NY: Yearling Books.

Steedman, Scott. 1997. *How Would You Survive as an American Indian?* San Francisco, CA: Children's Book Press.

Thomson, Peggy. 1995. *Katie Henio: Navajo Sheepherder*. New York, NY: Dutton Juvenille.

Vigina, Driving Hawk Sneve. 1994. *The Nez Perce: A First Americans Book*. New York, NY: Holiday House.

Grades 6–12

Alexie, Sherman. 2009. *The Absolutely True Diary of a Part-Time Indian*. New York, NY: Little, Brown Books for Young Readers.

Bierhorst, John, 2005. *In the Trail of the Wind: American Indian Poems and Ritual Orations*. New York, NY: Farrar, Straus, and Giroux.

Brown, Dee. 2007. *Bury My Heart at Wounded Knee: An Indian History of the American West*. New York, NY: Henry Holt and Company.

Carlson, Lori Marie. 2005. *Moccasin Thunder: American Indian Stories for Today*. New York, NY: HarperCollins Publishers.

Dewey, Jennifer. 2003. *Navajo Summer*. Honesdale, PA: Boyds Mills Press.

Frost, Helen. 2011. *Diamond Willow*. New York, NY: Square Fish.

Hamilton, Virginia. 1995. *Arilla Sun Down*. New York: Scholastic.

Highwater, Jamake. 1990. *Anapao: An American Indian Odyssey*. New York, NY: HarperCollins Publishers.

Murdoch, David. 2005. *North American Indian*. New York, NY: DK Children.

Asian Emphasis

Grades K–2

Baker, Keith. 1997. *The Magic Fan*. London: Sandpiper.

Breckler, Rosemary. 1992. *Hoang Breaks the Lucky Teapot*. Chicago: Houghton Mifflin Harcourt.

Brown, Don. 2008. *Bright Path: Young Jim Thorpe*. New York: NY: Square Fish.

Demi. 1995. *The Stonecutter*. New York, NY: Knopf Books for Young Readers.

Friedman, Ina. 1987. *How My Parents Learned to Eat*. Chicago: Houghton Mifflin Harcourt.

Haskins, James. 1987. *Count Your Way through China*. Minneapolis, MN: Lerner Publishing Group.

Hoyt-Goldsmith, Diane. 1998. *Celebrating Chinese New Year*. New York: Holiday House.

Kajikawa, Kimiko. 2000. *Yoshi's Feast*. New York, NY: DK Children.

Lee, Jeanne. 2002. *Bitter Dumplings*. New York: Farrar, Straus, and Giroux.

Lee, Huy Voun. 1998. *At the Beach*. New York, NY: Henry Holt and Company.

Lin, Grace. 2001. *Dim Sum for Everyone!* New York, NY: Knopf Books for Young Readers.

McCully Arnold, Emily. 1998. *Beautiful Warrior*. New York, NY: Arthur L. Levine Books.

Mosel, Arlene. 2007. *Tikki Tikki Tempo*. New York, NY: Square Fish.

Rattigan, Jama Kim. 1998. *Dumpling Soup*. New York, NY: Little, Brown Books for Young Readers.

Santore, Charles. 2007. *The Silk Princess*. New York: Random House Digital, Inc.

Wong, Janet. 2006. *Apple Pie 4th of July*. London: Sandpiper.

Yin. 2003. *Coolies*. London: Puffin Books.

Yolen, Jane. 1998. *The Emperor and the Kite*. London: Puffin Books.

Young, Ed. 1996. *Lon Po Po: A Red-Riding Hood Story from China*. London: Puffin Books.

———. 1998. *Cat and Rat: The Legend of the Chinese Zodiac*. New York: Henry Holt Books for Young Readers.

Grades 3–5

Lee, Milly. 2006. *Landed*. New York: Farrar, Straus, and Giroux.

Namioka, Lensey. 1994. *Yang the Youngest and his Terrible Ear*. New York, NY: Yearling.

———. 2004. *Half and Half*. New York, NY: Yearling.

Newman, Lesléa. 2008. *Hachiko Waits*. New York, NY: Square Fish.

Noguchi, Rich and Jenks, Deneen. 2001. *Flowers for Mariko*. New York, NY: Lee and Low Books.

Park, Linda Sue. 2008. *Archer's Quest*. New York, NY: Yearling Books.

———. 2009. *Seesaw Girl*. London: Sandpiper.

San Souci, Daniel. 1999. *In the Moonlight Mist: A Korean Tale*. Honesdale, PA: Boyds Mills Press.

Say, Allen. 1996. *El Chino*. London: Sandpiper.

Uchida, Yoshiko. 1993. *A Jar of Dreams*. New York, NY: Aladdin Paperbacks.

Wells, Ruth. 1990. *The Dragon Prince: A Chinese Beauty and the Beast Tale*. New York: HarperCollins.

———. 1992. *A to Zen: A Book of Japenese Culture*. New York: Simon and Schuster Books for Young Readers.

Yep, Laurence. 1996. *Hiroshima*. New York: Scholastic, Inc.

———. 2003. *The Magic Paintbrush*. New York, NY: HarperCollins Publishers.

Zhang, Song Nan. 1998. *The Ballad of Mulan*. Union City, CA: Pan Asian Publications.

Grades 6–12

Banerjee, Anjali. 2006. *Maya Running*. New York, NY: Laurel Leaf Books.

Chen, Da. 2004. *Wandering Warrior*. New York, NY: Laurel Leaf Books.

Crew, Linda. 1991. *Children of the River*. New York, NY: Laurel Leaf Books.

Fletcher, Susan. 1999. *Shadow Spinner*. New York, NY: Aladdin Paperbacks.

Jango-Cohen, Judith. 2005. *Chinese New Year*. Minneapolis, MN: Carolrhoda Books.

Kadohata, Cynthia. 2004. *Kira-Kira*. New York, NY: Atheneum Books.

Kleeman, Terry and Barrett, Tracy. 2005. *The Ancient Chinese World*. Oxford, UK: Oxford University Press.

Namioka, Lensey. 2006. *An Ocean Apart, A World Away*. New York, NY: Laurel Leaf Books.

Paulsen, Gary. 1991. *Canyons*. New York, NY: Laurel Leaf Books.

Salisbury, Graham. 2007. *Eyes of the Emperor*. New York, NY: Laurel Leaf Books.

Wong, Janet. 2008. *A Suitcase of Seaweed and Other Poems*. North Charleston, SC: Booksurge.

Yang, Gene Luen. 2008. *American Born Chinese*. New York, NY: Square Fish.

Yen Mah, Adeline. 2001. *Chinese Cinderella: The True Story of an Unwanted Daughter*. New York, NY: Laurel Leaf Books.

Appendix D

Culturally Responsive Read-Aloud Activities

Name: **Teacher Reads Aloud**	
Description: The teacher reads the text aloud, modeling the prosodic features of the language.	
How-To Steps: The students listen and follow along in their books while the teacher reads to students.	
Pros: All readers benefit from hearing a proficient reader: low affective filter.	**Cons:** The students may want to participate but are required to listen; lack of student participation.
What Makes It Culturally Responsive: In effect, when teachers read aloud, it has the same result as storytelling for students in their communities. Listening to an adult read an engaging story reminds students of having listened to a care provider at home tell a story.	

Name: **Train Reading (Proficient Readers Only Read)**	
Description: Just as a train has an engine, cars, and a caboose, the teacher starts as the first reader as the engine and chooses the proficient readers to be the cars and caboose.	
How-To Steps: The teacher chooses readers prior to the reading and when the teacher directs, the next student follows, and so on. Teacher chooses three to five students ahead of time and tells them that they will read when directed.	
Pros: Proficient readers can model fluency; prosodic features.	**Cons:** Struggling readers will want to read (need to increased fluency); lack of equitable participation.
What Makes It Culturally Responsive: Train Reading provides an opportunity for readers to accomplish a task together for a common purpose. Students who have this experience not only feel validated for their reading ability but also have a sense of identity that they are leaders in the class. This gets buy-in from the students who are affirmed and recognized for something they do well.	

Name: **Jump-In Reading**
Description: The students have the autonomy to choose when they would like to participate and read aloud by "jumping-in."
How-To Steps: The student reads, and another student can jump when there is a stop period. The student can stop and go with the silence (it's perfectly acceptable). Students must read at least one sentence, or they can read for as long as they want or until someone jumps in. Having moments of silence allows students to think and reflect about what was just read. If two or more jump in at the same time, one student shall defer to the other.

Pros: Highly engaging; low affective filter; student centered.	**Cons:** Struggling readers will want to read; lack of equitable participation.

What Makes It Culturally Responsive: Jump-In Reading simulates more naturally how a conversation occurs in some languages. The appropriate time to "jump in" during a conversation is culturally and linguistically based. The appropriate time to jump in during a conversation is different for various cultures. In the culture of school and mainstream culture, jumping in is considered rude and interrupting. Jump-In Reading is a build-and-bridge strategy that validates and affirms the home culture for transitioning to the culture of school.

Name: **Fade In and Fade Out**
Description: The teacher uses nonverbal cues to choose students to read. Students must be able to read and listen for another reader's cues.
How-To Steps: The teacher walks around the room and touches the shoulder of a student who starts to read with a whisper and gradually increases the volume to a normal reading voice. As the first student reads, the teacher touches another student's shoulder, and that student begins fade-in. The student who is reading then fades out, going from normal volume to a whisper. The reader starts to read over the first reader who begins to fade out.

Pros: Models fluency in a strong way.	**Cons:** High affective filter, students have little choice; struggling readers will want to read; lack of equitable participation.

What Makes It Culturally Responsive: Fade-In and Fade-Out reading gives an opportunity for students to work together toward a common goal.

Name: **Echo-Read**	
Description: The teacher reads and students echo.	
How-To Steps: The teacher reads one sentence, paragraph, or section then stops. Students echo the teacher by reading the same sentence in the same way.	
Pros: Great for modeling prosody; sense of cooperation; low affective filter.	**Cons:** Student participation
What Makes It Culturally Responsive: Echo-Read is a strategy that is often used with struggling readers. This strategy has a low affective filter, as students do not feel pressured to read correctly, as they just have to echo what they hear.	

Name: **Buddy Read (Paired Reading)**	
Description: Proficient readers read to nonproficient readers. This can be done with peers or pairing upper-grade students with lower-grade students, keeping the same buddy throughout the semester.	
How-To Steps: The teachers assign students as buddies who will read the text together. Proficient readers are paired with nonproficient readers to ensure that the text is being read by each group, even if it is one student reading and the other listening.	
Pros: The students are motivated to work with peers, engaging; low affective filter; student centered.	**Cons:** The teacher must actively check up on each group to ensure that students in pairs are reading.
What Makes It Culturally Responsive: Buddy Read gives students the opportunity to engage in text with another peer to create a fun experience while reading. Reading is not an isolating experience; rather, students have a peer with whom they can share a story.	

Name: **Choral Reading**	
Description: All the students, lead by the teacher, read aloud together.	
How-To Steps: Just as a choir sings in unison, the teacher leads the students to read together in one voice. The teacher points out where to start in the passage and cues students to read. All students are expected to read together in unison.	
Pros: Low affective filter	**Cons:** Student engagement
What Makes It Culturally Responsive: Choral Reading provides students with the opportunity to read collaboratively.	

Name: **Radio Reading**	
Description: Proficient readers are chosen to read a text with different voices. They can choose an emotion to relay, such as *happy*, *sad*, *sleepy*, or they can choose a voice type, such as an old woman or a baby.	
How-To Steps: The teacher must choose proficient readers that read expressively beforehand so the student can practice their voice of choice.	
Pros: High engagement	**Cons:** Limited to proficient readers; possible to lose track of story line and focus on the reader.
What Makes It Culturally Responsive: Radio Reading provides students with the opportunity to showcase a talent and affirm something they are good at. Also, shows that reading can be fun and enjoyable, and can lead to dramatic interpretation, which many students have an affinity toward.	

Appendix E

Culturally Responsive Literacy Strategy Activities

Literacy Strategy Activity: Language Experience Approach for Sight-Word Development

CR Element(s): Preference for context-based (field dependent) learning structures

Steps:

1. Individually or in groups, students dictate a story as the teacher records it. The written story is based on the students' oral language and personal experience, whether built by the teacher or already possessed by the students. These features of language experience increase the likelihood that students, particularly low-achieving readers, will be able to read and comprehend the dictated text, since the words are their own and not those of another writer, which may or may not correspond with the students' experiences, culturally or linguistically.

2. When the dictation is completed, the teacher should read the dictated story aloud and point to each word as students follow along. This procedure further helps to build a sight-word vocabulary for words that students already possess as part of a speaking vocabulary but have not yet learned in their written form. As the teacher reads the story, learners should be given an opportunity to make any changes.

3. Once changes are completed, the teacher and students read the story together, with the teacher again pointing with smooth motion at each word as it is read.

4. Students now try reading the story alone. If there are any words at this point that they cannot pronounce, the teacher should note these for later practice and review. These words might go into a personal word bank or word wall that may serve as individual dictionaries for future reference for reading or for writing stories.

5. When the teacher feels confident that students have mastered the words as sight words for the dictated story, a final activity could be to have the story rewritten as an additional summary and illustrated with a picture, if students so desire.

Recommended Uses: Word recognition and vocabulary

Literacy Strategy Activity: Phonograms—Hink-Pinks, Hinky-Pinkies, Hinkety-Pinketies

CR Element(s): Preference for rhythmic and sociocentric learning activities

Steps:

1. Before reading, the teacher uses a picture walk to introduce a book that incorporates multiple rhyming words.

2. The teacher encourages students to listen to the story and explains that they are going to be listening for words that sound alike at the end, such as *frog* and *log*. The teacher reads the story while the class listens.

3. During reading, the teacher briefly pauses several times to get the students to name a word that rhymes with a word from the story.

4. After reading, the teacher explains that he or she is going to give some clues and the class will have to think of rhyming words to guess the riddle. At least one of the words the students will be guessing should come from the story. For example, if the book included a fish, one clue and answer could be *a dream or request made by a water animal from our story*. (fish/wish)

5. For those learners having difficulty guessing the answers to the riddles, the teacher can provide one of the words in the hink pink (the rhyming words that answer the clue) and the students can guess the second rhyming word.

6. The teacher could begin with the riddles in this way to provide scaffolding. Gradually, the teacher would give the clues as written and let the class guess both rhyming words. Eventually, students can create their own riddles with rhyming words as answers.

7. Pairs of words that are one-syllable answers to riddles are called *hink-pinks*, while answers of two syllables are called *hinky-pinkies*, and three-syllable answers are called *hinkety-pinketies*. (For example: *frog-log* (hink-pink), *gory-story* (hinky-pinky), and *robbery-snobbery* (hinkety-pinkety)

Recommended Uses: Postreading, word recognition, and vocabulary building

Literacy Strategy Activity: Thinking Maps

CR Element(s): Provides support for inductive learning by making concept relationships explicit.

Overview:

Thinking Maps are visual organizers that are used consistently to frame seven particular types of thinking. They differ from graphic organizers in that they should be used exclusively to organize the types of thinking most often required in an educational setting:

- defining in context
- comparing and contrasting
- categorizing and classifying
- making or recognizing analogies
- understanding whole-to-part relationships
- describing
- recognizing cause-and-effect/problem-and-solution relationships

They also differ from graphic organizers in that they are flexible (i.e., adjustable to an activity, and students are able to draw them independently). Students who are proficient with Thinking Maps can identify the type of Thinking Map (e.g., visual, needed to represent the type of thinking an activity requires and create it accordingly).

Recommended Uses: Before, during, and after reading

Literacy Strategy Activity: Reader's Theater

CR Element(s): Preference for sociocentric learning environments and performance-based kinesthetic activities

Overview: Reader's Theater involves students in oral reading through reading parts in scripts. It helps with building fluency through oral reading.

Recommended Uses: During and after reading

Literacy Strategy Activity: SQ3R

CR Element(s): Provides support for inductive learning by structuring how to identify and remember important information

Overview:

SQ3R stands for

- **Survey**: The reader previews the material to develop a general outline for organizing information.

- **Question**: The reader raises questions with the expectation of finding answers in the material to be studied.

- **Read**: The reader next attempts to answer the questions formulated in the previous step.

- **Recite**: The reader then deliberately attempts to answer out loud or in writing the questions formulated in the second step.

- **Review**: The reader finally reviews the material by rereading portions of the assignment in order to verify the answers given during the previous step.

Steps:

1. Lead students in a survey of a reading selection. Pay special attention to headings, subheadings, topic sentences, and highlighted words.

2. Build a question for each heading and subheading in the text selection. These questions will be answered during the reading of the text.

3. Ask students to read the selection carefully, keeping the questions in mind as they read.

4. Have students "recite" the answers to the questions by verbalizing them in a group discussion or writing them down. This act of restating thought in spoken or written form reinforces learning.

5. Repeat this process for all of the questions.

6. Finally, have students review all of their spoken or written answers. Once SQ3R has been modeled several times to students, the teacher can provide students with the SQ3R Guide Sheet. This worksheet contains the cues to be used at each step.

Recommended Uses: Before, during, and after reading expository text

Literacy Strategy Activity: Reciprocal Teaching

CR Element(s): Preference for cooperative and sociocentric learning environments

Overview:

Reciprocal teaching refers to an instructional activity that takes place in the form of a dialogue between teachers and students (and eventually among students) regarding segments of text. The dialogue is structured by the use of four strategies:

- summarizing
- question generating
- clarifying
- predicting

The teacher and students take turns assuming the role of the teacher in leading this dialogue. The purpose of reciprocal teaching is to facilitate a group effort between teacher and students as well as among students in the task of bringing meaning to the text. Each strategy was selected for the following purpose:

Summarizing provides the opportunity to identify and integrate the most important information in the text.	**Question generating** reinforces the summarizing strategy and carries the learner one more step along in the comprehension activity.
Steps:	**Steps:**
1. Distribute selected text to students.	1. Have students identify the kind of information that is significant in the text to provide the substance for a question.
2. Encourage students to summarize across sentences, paragraphs, and the passage as a whole.	2. Have students create questions and a self-test to ascertain that they can indeed answer their own questions.
When students first begin the reciprocal-teaching procedure, their efforts are generally focused at the sentence and paragraph levels. As they become more proficient, they are able to integrate at the paragraph and passage levels.	Question generating is a flexible strategy to the extent that students can be taught and encouraged to generate questions at many levels.

Clarifying is an activity that is particularly important when working with students who have a history of comprehension difficulty.

Steps:

1. Explain to students that the purpose of reading is not to say the words correctly and that it is acceptable if the text does not make sense to them.

2. Remind students that when they are asked to clarify, their attention is called to the fact that there may be many reasons why text is difficult to understand (e.g., new vocabulary, unclear reference words, difficult concepts).

Clarifying alerts to the effects of such impediments to comprehension and to take the necessary measures to restore meaning.

Predicting occurs when students hypothesize what the author will discuss next in the text.

Steps:

1. Review the relevant background knowledge that students already possess regarding the topic of study.

2. Explain to students that they have a purpose for reading: to confirm or disprove their hypothesis. Tell students that they will be able to link their new knowledge with the knowledge they already possess.

The predicting strategy also facilitates use of text structure as students learn that headings, subheadings, and questions embedded in the text are useful means of anticipating what might occur next.

Recommended Uses: Before, during, and after reading

Literacy Strategy Activity: Anticipation/Reaction Guide

CR Element(s): Preference for sociocentric learning activities

Overview:

An Anticipation/Reaction Guide utilizes a twin strategy to increase reading comprehension. It stimulates prior knowledge and experiences before reading and then reinforces key concepts after reading.

- The guide presents students with a series of leading questions to be answered in writing before reading.

- Students then share their answers in a class discussion designed specifically to activate, or better reactivate, prior knowledge. This review of prior knowledge helps students to connect with the topic.

- Students read the text passage and then evaluate their written answers (prior knowledge). Students should note when their answers agree or disagree with the text's content.

- Finally, students engage in a summarizing discussion, expressing how the reading selection reinforced or challenged their prior knowledge.

Steps:

1. Outline the main ideas in a reading selection. Write the ideas in a short list (no more than five or six points), using clear declarative statements. Do not include generalizations or abstractions in this list.

2. Rewrite the main statements in the form of questions to prompt the students' prior knowledge and to elicit student reactions and predictions.

3. Have students write responses to each of the questions. These written responses should include any necessary explanation or evidence.

4. Allow students to openly discuss their answers/predictions prior to reading. Note any recurring themes in the discussion. Also, note any opposing or contradictory points of view.

5. Have students read the selected passage. Instruct students to make comments on their written answer sheet, noting agreement and disagreement between their answers and the author's message or purpose.

Recommended Uses: Before and after reading

Literacy Strategy Activity: ORDER

CR Element(s): Provides support for inductive learners with strategies for making text structure explicit

Overview: ORDER is an acronym for

- **O**pen your mind

- **R**ecognize the structure

- **D**raw an organizer

- **E**xplain it

- **R**euse it

The ORDER strategy recognizes both the power of graphical organizers to assist students in visualizing the organization of information in a reading selection and the importance of independent, unguided student thought. This strategy calls for students rather than teachers to produce graphic organizers.

These student-produced organizers take two forms. If the student recognizes one of the common organizational structures—enumeration/description, time order/sequence, compare/contrast, cause/effect, or problem/solution—in a document, he or she may choose to employ one of the standard graphical organizer forms. If none of the common structures are applicable, then the student builds a custom form to visually represent the organization of ideas in a document.

Steps:
1. Select a document for students to read. Ask students to take notes on the key concepts and structure of the document. Have them produce a simple outline of the document's contents.

2. Ask students to evaluate the document's organization against the five standard organizational patterns. If the organization matches one of these patterns, have students complete the corresponding visual organizer or Thinking Map to visually represent the document's content and structure. If the organization does not match any of the standard patterns, encourage students to build their own graphical representation of the document's structure.

3. Open a class discussion to compare student conclusions. If students disagree on the best organizer to describe the document's organization, have them explain each viewpoint and defend it with evidence from the text.

Recommended Uses: Before, during, after reading

Literacy Strategy Activity: Hot Seat

CR Element(s): Preference for sociocentric and performance-based learning activities

Steps:

1. Students read part or all of a selected piece of literature.

2. Divide the class into groups of 3–5 students. Each student selects a character whose persona he or she will adopt and prepares for an interrogation from the rest of the class.

3. Have all students (working independently or in small groups) prepare questions for each character. Questions may focus on recalling the story or deal with a character's emotions. Hot Seat formats vary with the group of students. Teachers may ask a panel of characters to assume the "hot seat" or limit it to individuals. Variation: Use puppets, character masks, or murals as a lead-in.

Recommended Uses: After reading

Literacy Strategy Activity: Can You Feel Me?

CR Element(s): Preference for interpersonal, sociocentric, and affective learning activities

Overview:

This strategy gives validity to students' personal reactions to selected pieces of writing, allows students to express their reactions in a nonjudgmental setting; draws images together from all points of the poem, story, or prose; and allows students to reflect and select unforgettable mental pictures.

Steps:

1. Have students read the selected text silently and independently.

2. Tell students to select and highlight words, phrases, or sentences that they find particularly meaningful or that create vivid mental images.

3. Invite students to participate in a voluntary, random sharing of their selected images from the literature. They read aloud, "as the spirit moves them."

4. Explain to students that as one person reads, everyone should be listening.

5. Take active participation in this activity and allow for possible periods of silence.

Optional extensions: Students may record their selections in a double-entry journal, illustrate their mental pictures, and/or write about and share the importance of their particular selection.

Recommended Uses: After reading

Literacy Strategy Activity: Tea Party

CR Element(s): Preference for interpersonal sociocentric kinesthetic learning activities

Steps:

A Tea Party serves as a valuable "intro" activity before students even see the book and gives the students a "taste" of the book, novel, or play.

1. Distribute quotes from the text and revisit them in context during the actual reading, providing many opportunities for an "Ah-ha!"

2. Encourage students to share their thoughts.

Recommended Uses: Before reading

Suggested Writing Activities

Acrostics: Poems created by writing a name or concept down the left side of a page. For each letter, write a word or phrase that describes the name or concept to you.

Alternative Endings: Students develop a new ending for a written or oral story.

Brainstorming: Students are given a topic that they discuss with peers in a small group. They use the language that is most comfortable for them. As ideas arise, students record the ideas in standard-language form. The teacher facilitates a whole-group discussion of the topic, using standard language.

Character Portraits: Concentrating on the roles of specific characters, students create pictures of the characters and describe how they fit into the story.

Character Profiles: Students develop a short description of a character, using nonstandard language and/or standard language.

Culture Bits: Short bits of cultural information are provided to students at the beginning, the middle, or the end of class. Students must take notes and discuss the cultural topic.

Dictation: The teacher selects a passage and reads it three times, first at normal speed, then a little slower, and finally at normal speed again. Students listen to the first reading, write the sentence(s) during the second reading, and confirm their recorded sentence(s) as they listen to the third reading.

Discovery Words: Word-webs concept; circles of words that are acquired outside of the school setting.

Draw It: Teachers choose a target sentence from a reading selection; students write the selected sentence and their meaning of the sentence and draw a pictorial representation.

Interviews: Students prepare a set of open-ended questions revolving around a cultural topic. They use the questions to interview people within their family and community.

Journal Writing: Students engage in free writing about a specific topic or a meaningful experience in either nonstandard or standard language.

Predicting: Students consider what will occur next in a reading selection and write their predictions in their own words and/or translate their prediction in standard-language form.

Question Circle: Students are seated in a circle. Each student has a sheet of paper and writes a question at the top of that paper. They then pass their paper to the left. Each student answers the question on the sheet they receive.

Scrambled Sentences: Students rearrange a list of scrambled words to form a sentence that makes sense.

Story-Retelling: Students retell a story in oral or written form using nonstandard language or standard language. They may share their retelling with a partner.

Summarizing: Students write a short description of a reading selection. The summary can also be provided orally.

Appendix

G

CLR Learning
Environment Survey

CLR Learning Environment Survey

Teacher _____ **Grade/Class** _____

Observer _____ **Date of Observation** _____

Observe the learning environment in your colleague's classroom by rating its cultural responsiveness on two levels:

- **Quantitative:** Is the environmental feature in place? Yes or No
- **Qualitative:** aspects of responsiveness, including creativity, presentation, and student friendliness

Rate the quality of responsiveness on a five-point scale from very responsive (5) to least responsive (1).

Add comments or suggestions to discuss with the teacher whose classroom you have observed.

Print-Rich Environment

Quantitative: Is the 70:30 ratio of authentic to commercially produced print resources evident in the classroom?

Yes or No (circle one)

Qualitative: Rate the level responsiveness (creativity, presentation, and student friendliness)

Very Responsive				**Least Responsive**
5	4	3	2	1

Comments/Suggestions:

_____

_____

_____

Learning Centers

Quantitative: Are a variety of learning centers present? Is space set up for them to be organized?

Yes or No (circle one)

Qualitative: Rate the level of responsiveness (creativity, presentation, and student friendliness)

Very Responsive   **Least Responsive**
   5   4   3   2   1

Comments/Suggestions:

_____

_____

_____

Culturally Colorful

Quantitative: Does the room feature a variety of colors that are relevant to various cultures or to the culture/activities of the school?

Yes or No (circle one)

Qualitative: Rate the level responsiveness (creativity, presentation, and student friendliness)

Very Responsive   **Least Responsive**
   5   4   3   2   1

Comments/Suggestions:

_____

_____

_____

Optimally Arranged

Quantitative: Does the room arrangement facilitate ease of movement, management, and presentations?

Yes or No (circle one)

Qualitative: Rate the level responsiveness (creativity, presentation, and student friendliness)

Very Responsive   **Least Responsive**

   5   4   3   2   1

Comments/Suggestions:

_____

_____

_____

Multiple Libraries

Quantitative: Do the library resources support a focus on multiple literacies and cultures?

Yes or No (circle one)

Qualitative: Rate the level responsiveness (creativity, presentation, and student friendliness)

Very Responsive   **Least Responsive**

   5   4   3   2   1

Comments/Suggestions:

_____

_____

_____

Technology

Quantitative: Are technology resources present and ready for use?

Yes or No (circle one)

Qualitative: Rate the level responsiveness (creativity, presentation, and student friendliness)

Very Responsive   **Least Responsive**
    5   4   3   2   1
Comments/Suggestions:

_____

_____

_____

Relevant Bulletin Boards

Quantitative: Are the bulletin boards relevant to the content areas and the cultural diversity of the students?

Yes or No (circle one)

Qualitative: Rate the level responsiveness (creativity, presentation, and student friendliness)

Very Responsive   **Least Responsive**
    5   4   3   2   1
Comments/Suggestions:

_____

_____

_____

Plan for Using Survey Findings

What are the strengths in the learning environment?

_____
_____
_____
_____
_____
_____
_____

What are the limitations in the learning environment?

_____
_____
_____
_____
_____
_____
_____

What are your plans for using the survey findings?

_____
_____
_____
_____
_____
_____
_____
_____

References Cited

Allen, J. 1999. *Words, words, words*. Portland, ME: Stenhouse Publishers.

Anderson, J. A. 1995. Literacy and education in the African-American experience. In *Literacy among African-American youth*, eds. V. L. Gadsen and D. A. Wagner, 27. Cresskill: Hampton.

Baugh, J. 2004. Standard English and academic English (dialect) learners in the African diaspora. *Journal of English Linguistics* 32(3): 198–209.

Beck, I. L., M. G. McKeown, and L. Kucan. 2002. *Bringing words to life*. New York: The Guilford Press.

Blachowicz C., and P. Fisher. 2006. *Teaching vocabulary in all classrooms*. Upper Saddle River, NJ: Pearson Education.

Bromley, K. 2007. Nine things every teacher should know about words and vocabulary instruction. *Journal of Adolescent & Adult Literacy* 50 (7): 528–537.

Brooks, G. 1966. "We real cool." In *The poetry of Black America: Anthology of the twentieth century*, ed. Arnold Adoff. New York: Harper Teen, 1973.

Corson, D. 1997. Non-standard varieties and educational policy. In *Encyclopedia of language and education,* ed. R. Wodak abd D. Corson, Vol. 1, 99–109. Dordrecht, Netherlands: Kluwer Academic Publishers.

Cronbach, L. J. 1942. An analysis of techniques for diagnostic vocabulary testing. *Journey of Educational Research* 36(3), 206–217.

Danielson, C. 2007. *Enhancing professional practice: a framework for teaching*. Alexandria, VA: Association for Supervision & Curriculum Development.

Delpit, L., and J. K. E. Dowdy. 2002. *The skin that we speak.* New York: The New Press.

Dillard, J. L. 1972. *Black English: Its history and usage in the United States.* New York: Random.

Emmer, E. T. , C.M. Evertson, and M.E. Worsham. 2003. *Classroom management for secondary teachers* (6th ed.). Boston: Allyn & Bacon.

Feldman, K. and K. Kinsella. 2003. Narrowing the language gap: Strategies for vocabulary development. www.fcoe.net/ela/pdf/vocabulary/narrowing⁄20vocab⁄20gap⁄20KK⁄20KF⁄201.pdf (accessed August 2, 2001).

Fought, C. 2003. *Chicano English in context.* Great Britain: Palgrave Macmillan.

Frayer, D. A., W. D. Frederick, and J. J. Klaumeier. 1969. A schema for testing the level of concept mastery. *Working paper No. 16.* Madison, WI: Wisconsin Research and Development Center for Cognitive Learning.

Gardner-Chloros. 2009. *Codeswitching*. Cambridge: Cambridge University Press.

Gay, G. 2000. *Culturally responsive teaching: Theory, research, and practice.* New York: Teachers College Press.

Gonzales, A. E. 1922. *The Black Border: Gullah stories of the Carolina Coast.* Columbia SC: The State Company.

Good, T. L., and J. E. Brophy. 1977. *Educational pyschology: A realistic approach.* New York: Holt, Rinehart & Winston.

Goodwin. 2008, December 1. *Changing the odds for children at-risk.* http://www.newamerica.net/events/2008/.changing_odds, accessed June 22, 2011.

Graves, M. F. 2006. *The vocabulary book: Learning & instruction.* New York: Teachers College Press.

Graves, M. F., and S. Watts-Taffe. 2002. The place of word consciousness in a research-based vocabulary program. *What research has to say about reading instruction, 3rd edition,* eds. A. E. Farstrup and S. J. Samuels, 140–165. Newark, DE: International Reading Association.

Hale-Benson, J. 1986. *Black children: Their roots, culture and learning styles.* Rev. ed. Baltimore: Johns Hopkins University Press.

Harris, V. 1999. *Teaching multicultural literature in grades K–8.* Norwood, MA: Christopher-Gordon Publishers, Inc.

Herskovits, M. J. 1941. *Myth of the Negro past.* Massachusetts, Beacon Press.

Hollins, E. R. 2008. *Culture in school learning: Revealing the deep meaning.* Mahwah NJ: Erlbaum.

Hooks, B. 2003. *Rock my soul: Black people and self-esteem*: New York: Atria.

Hughes, L. 1951. *Montage of a Dream Deferred: Selected poems of Langston Hughes.* New York: Vintage. 1990.

Irvine, J. J. 1991. *Black students and school failure.* New York: Praeger.

Jackson, R. R. 2009. *Never work harder than your students & other principles of great teaching.* Alexandria, VA: Association for Supervision and Curriculum Development.

Jackson, Y. 2009. Fearless leading. *Educational Leadership*, 67(2), 34–39.

Jensen, E. 2005. *Teaching with the brain in mind,* 2nd edition. Alexandria, VA: Association for Supervision and Curriculum Development.

Johnson, D. W., R. T. Johnson, and E. J. Holubec. 1994. *Cooperative learning in the classroom.* Alexandria, VA: Association for Supervision & Curriculum Development.

Kagan, S., and M. Kagan. 2009. *Kagan cooperative learning.* San Clemente, CA: Kagan Publishing.

Kotulak, R. 1996. *Inside the brain: Revolutionary discoveries of how the mind works.* Kansas City: Andrew McMeel.

Krashen, S. 2004. *The power of reading: Insights from the research.* Portsmouth, NH: Heinemann.

Labov, W. 1972. Academic ignorance and Black intelligence. *Atlantic Monthly*, June.

Ladson-Billings, G. 1994. *The dreamkeepers: Successful teachers of African American children*. San Francisco: Jossey-Bass.

Leap, W. L. 1993. *American Indian English*. Salt Lake City: University of Utah Press.LeMoine, N. 1999. *English for your success*. Maywood: People's Publishing.

LeMoine, N.R. 1999. *Understanding gene therapy*. New York,NY: BIOS Scientific Publishers

Levine, M. 2002. *A mind at a time*. New York: Simon & Schuster.

Marzano, R. (ed.) 2010. *On excellence in teaching*. Bloomington, IN: Solution Tree Press.

Marzano, R. J. 2009. *Designing and teaching learning goals and objectives: Classroom strategies that work*. Bloomington, IN: Solution Tree Press.

Marzano, R. J., J. S. Marzano, and D. J. Pickering. 2003. *Classroom management that works: Research-based strategies for every teacher*. Alexandria, VA: Association for Supervision & Curriculum Development.

Merriam-Webster Online Dictionary. 2011. http://www.merriam-webster.com/

Moos, R. H. 1979. *Evaluating educational environments*. San Francisco: JosseyBass.

Murphy, M. 2009. *Tools & talk: Data, conversation, and action for classroom and school improvement*. Oxford, OH: National Council of Staff Development (NCSD).

National Reading Panel. 2000. *Report of the National Reading Panel: Teaching children to read. Report of the subgroups*. Washington, DC: U.S. Department of Health and Human Services, National Institutes of Health.

Nieto, Sonia. 1999. *The light in their eyes: Creating multicultural learning communities*. New York: Teachers College Press.

Nobles, W. W. 1987. Psychometrics and African American Reality: A Question of Cultural Antimony, *Negro Educational Review*, 38 (2-3): 45–55.

Ogbu, J. U. 1978. *Minority educations and caste: The American system in cross cultural perspective.* New York: Academic Press.

Ramirez, M., and A. Castaneda. 1974. *Cultural democracy, by cognitive development and education.* New York: Academic Press.

Rasinski, T., N. Padak, R. M. Newton, and E. Newton. 2007. *Greek & Latin roots: Key to building vocabulary.* Huntington Beach, CA: Shell Education.

Richardson, J. 2006. Snapshots of learning. *Tools for Schools* 10(1): 1–3.

Shade, B., C. Kelly, and M. Oberg. 1997. *Creating culturally responsive classrooms.* Psychology in the classroom: A series on applied educational psychology, Viii, 168. Washington, DC: American Psychological Association.

Smith, E. A. 1992. African-American language behavior: A world of difference. Paper presented at the Claremont Reading Conference, Claremont, CA.

Smith, H. L. 1998. Literacy and instruction in African American communities: Shall we overcome. In *Sociocultural contexts of language and literacy*, ed. B. Perez. Mahwah, pp. 189–222. NJ: Lawrence Erlbaum Associates.

Smitherman, G. 1998. Ebonics, King, and Oakland: Some folk don't believe fat meat *is* greasy. *Journal of English Linguistics* 26 (2): 97–107.

Spring, J. 1994. *Deculturalization and the struggle for equality: A brief history of the education of dominated cultures in the United States.* New York: McGraw-Hill.

Stahl, S. A. 1999. *Vocabulary development.* Cambridge, MA: Brookline Books.

Syrus, P. First century B.C. ThinkExist.com, 2011, "Speech quotes." http://en.thinkexist.com/quotations/speech/2.html, accessed June 22, 2011.

Trelease, J. 2001. *The read-aloud handbook.* New York: Penguin Books.

Valenzuela, A. 1999. *Subtractive schooling: U.S.-Mexican youth and the politics of caring*. Albany, NY: State University of New York Press.

Villegas, A. M., and T. Lucas. 2007. The culturally responsive teacher. *Educational Leadership* 64 (6): 28–33.

Wilhelm, J. D. 2007. Imagining a new kind of self: Academic language, identity, and content area learning. *Voices from the Middle* 15 (1): 44–45.

Williams, J. D. 1990. *Literacy and bilingualism*. New York: Longman Press.

Williams, R. L. 1975. *Ebonics: The true language of black folks*. St. Louis: Institute of Black Studies.

Wolfe, P. 2001. *Brain matters: Translating research into classroom practice*. Alexandria, VA: Association for Supervision & Curriculum Development.

Yopp, R. H., and H. K. Yopp. 2007. Ten important words plus: A strategy for building word knowledge. *The Reading Teacher* 61(2): 157–160.

Through my work in preservice and inservice teacher development, I am acutely aware of the need for an effective pedagogical orientation that enables teachers of diverse student populations to appreciate and optimize all the resources their students bring to the classroom—cultural, linguistic, and academic. With this book, Sharroky Hollie provides the field with a culturally responsive approach to teaching enhanced with the additional lens of linguistically responsive practices that are relevant and rigorous.

—Dolores Beltran, P.h.D Consultant, Author, and Professor of the Master of Arts in Teaching Program at the University of Southern California

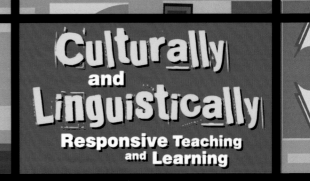

Culturally and Linguistically Responsive Teaching and Learning

*C*ulturally and Linguistically Responsive Teaching and Learning: Classroom Practices for Student Success provides educators with a pedagogical framework for infusing the most appropriate, engaging, and responsive teaching practices into today's diverse classrooms. This resource provides concrete practical activities and easy-to-implement strategies that address culture and language in five key areas: classroom management, academic literacy, academic vocabulary, academic language, and learning environment. Educators will feel empowered and excited to implement this framework, because it embraces and places value on students' culture and language, allowing them to thrive in the classroom.

Sharroky Hollie, Ph.D., is an assistant professor at California State University, Dominguez Hills. He is a cofounder of the nationally acclaimed Culture and Language Academy of Success in Los Angeles and the executive director of the Center for Culturally Responsive Teaching and Learning.

SHELL EDUCATION

ISBN 978-1-4258-0686-6

52499

9 781425 806866

SEP 50686 $24.99